PLANNING
EFFECTIVE
INSTRUCTION

PLANNING EFFECTIVE INSTRUCTION

Walter Dick
Robert A. Reiser

Florida State University

PRENTICE HALL, Englewood Cliffs, New Jersey 07632

Library of Congress Cataloging-in-Publication Data

Dick, Walter, (date)
  Planning effective instruction/Walter Dick and Robert A. Reiser.
    p.   cm.
  Includes index.
  ISBN 0-13-679457-2
  1. Instructional systems—United States. 2. Curriculum planning—
United States. I. Reiser, Robert A. II. Title.
LB1028.35.D5 1989
370'.7'32—dc19

88-25577
CIP

Cover design: *Diane Saxe*
Manufacturing buyer: *Peter Havens*

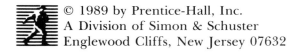 © 1989 by Prentice-Hall, Inc.
A Division of Simon & Schuster
Englewood Cliffs, New Jersey 07632

Printed in the United States of America

10 9 8 7 6 5 4 3 2 1

ISBN 0-13-679457-2

Prentice-Hall International (UK) Limited, *London*
Prentice-Hall of Australia Pty. Limited, *Sydney*
Prentice-Hall Canada Inc., *Toronto*
Prentice-Hall Hispanoamericana, S.A., *Mexico*
Prentice-Hall of India Private Limited, *New Delhi*
Prentice-Hall of Japan, Inc., *Tokyo*
Simon & Schuster Asia Pte. Ltd., *Singapore*
Editora Prentice-Hall do Brasil, Ltda., *Rio de Janeiro*

CONTENTS

PREFACE

Our motivation for writing this book was to provide teachers with a set of instructional planning skills to develop more effective instructional practices with the eventual result of greater student achievement. These planning skills have been used with great success by people who systematically design instructional materials. However, our goal was not to teach teachers to become instructional designers but rather to have teachers use some of the procedures and techniques that designers use to create effective instruction. We have attempted to provide skills that can be applied realistically within elementary and secondary classrooms without any special equipment or aids.

This text can be used in any of several teacher preparation courses. It may be used in a generic introductory course, or it may be used in a content-specific teacher education course. In the latter case the instructor would supplement the examples provided in the text with those that are most appropriate to the content area in which the students will become teachers. Lastly, the text may be effectively used in courses for inservice teachers who are looking for a new perspective on their classroom teaching activities.

To make it easier to learn from our text, we have used a standard format for each chapter. This format is described in detail in Chapter 1.

Each chapter contains an Application section that describes activities for a cumulative project. We encourage consideration of these activities because the true strength of the ideas that are being presented is most apparent in their application. It is our belief that the best understanding of the concepts in this book will come about from their use.

We have tried, in developing this book, to be faithful to our own design model. Nowhere was this more important than in our use of tryout and revision procedures. After the initial draft of the book was completed, we used it in a variety of ways. First, we met each week with two undergraduate students who read and critiqued the text, chapter by chapter, with us. We acknowledge the insightful comments of Teresa Robson and Bill Perry, who certainly gave us a better look at the instructional design process from the point of view of preservice teachers.

In addition, Barbara Brinson and Catherine Price used a draft of the text with their students at Southern Methodist University and Valdosta State College, respectively. Their feedback, along with that of their students, was invaluable to us. We also want to thank the following reviewers who gave us detailed critiques of an early draft of the text: Joann Bush, Juanita Cox, Judith Duffield, Debby King, Jim Klein, Marty Tessmer, and Karyn Wellhousen-Pugh. These various reviews resulted in a text that was substantially changed in a number of ways—all of which we believe are for the better. We gratefully acknowledge the value of this feedback, while retaining responsibility for the errors of omission and commission that may remain.

Our final gratitude is expressed to Lucy McGriff, our word processor, whose commitment to producing this text resulted in long hours of work at times when she would rather have been doing other things. To her we express our sincere appreciation.

W. D.
R.A.R.

CHAPTER ONE
WHAT IS EFFECTIVE INSTRUCTION?

What is it like to be a teacher? What is a teacher expected to do each day? An educator described the role of the classroom teacher as follows:

> The classroom, located within the larger school organization, is a crowded setting in which the teacher has to manage twenty-five or more students of approximately the same age who involuntarily spend—depending upon their grade level—anywhere from one to five hours daily in a room. Amidst continual communication with individual students and groups (up to 1,000 interactions a day in an elementary classroom), the teacher is expected to maintain control, teach a prescribed content, capture student interest in that content, match levels of instruction to differences among students, and show tangible evidence that students have performed satisfactorily.[*]

We believe that this description is an accurate one and points to the difficult tasks teachers face each day. How can a teacher perform these tasks successfully? We certainly do not have all the answers to this question. However, in the last twenty years, new ideas have emerged and new methods have been developed for planning and delivering instruction. The use of these ideas and methods has often resulted in the kind of learning we

[*]Larry Cuban. *Teachers and Machines*. New York: Teachers College Press, 1986. pp. 57–58.

1

would like to see take place with students. The purpose of this book is to help you learn about these ideas and methods, and to give you opportunities to use them. We believe that if you employ the ideas and methods described in this book, you will be a teacher whose instructional practices are effective.

DEFINING OUR TERMS

It is important that we are particularly clear in what we mean by the term "effective instruction," as used in the title of this book. Effective instruction is instruction that enables students to acquire specified skills, knowledge, and attitudes. Effective instruction is also instruction that students enjoy.

How can we judge whether instruction is effective? If you reexamine our definition of effective instruction, you will see that we can't make a judgment based on what the teacher does. Rather, we must make a judgment based upon what students are able to do and how they feel as a result of the instruction they receive.

We can use a variety of ways to determine what students can do. For example, school districts often use standardized tests that have been developed by testing experts. At other times it is quite possible to use tests that have been developed by a local school district or by a classroom teacher. To determine how students feel about instruction, an important indicator is their reaction to questions we ask them about the instructional process.

Effective instruction is determined on the basis of data and information that are gathered and documented. It is not based upon casual observation of what might be going on in the classroom. Consider a type of elementary school teacher whom we have all known at some time during our years in school. This teacher often takes students on field trips to the mall and to other interesting local sites. The teacher provides lots of time at recess, often meets with parents and tells them how well their children are doing, and is generally acknowledged to be a very loving and supportive teacher. It is very difficult to be critical of a person like this, a teacher who seems to possess many of the qualities of a "good teacher."

However, it is also necessary to ask what students learn as a result of having spent a year with such a teacher. To what extent has their knowledge base increased? How many new skills have they acquired? Have they sharpened some of the skills they already possessed, and have their attitudes toward learning improved? If the answers to these questions can be documented in a positive fashion, we applaud such a teacher for having delivered effective instruction. If, however, there have been no changes in the level of student performance or attitudes, we have to wonder about the effectiveness of the instruction these students have received.

How does a teacher go about planning for effective instruction? It doesn't just happen; an instructional plan must be carefully considered. The elements that are part of the instructional plan are derived primarily from a process called instructional design.

INSTRUCTIONAL DESIGN IN THE TEACHING PROCESS

Instructional design, which has emerged over the last twenty years, is a process used primarily to develop a wide variety of instructional materials, such as printed materials, computer-assisted instruction, and televised instruction. Research has shown that this process is an effective means of planning any type of instruction. A formal definition of instructional design is: a systematic process for designing, developing, implementing, and evaluating instruction. While the word *design* is repeated in the definition, it is used to represent the entire process as well.

Our intent is not to try to convince you to become an instructional designer, for instructional designers usually spend the majority of their time planning and developing instruction. They typically spend a relatively small portion of their time directly interacting with students. In contrast, you, as a teacher, will be spending most of your professional time interacting with students. Although the amount of time you will have for planning will be somewhat limited, we believe that the quality of your interactions with students will be greatly enhanced if you spend time employing some of the planning techniques used by instructional designers.

An instructional plan consists of a number of components that, when integrated, provide you with an outline for delivering effective instruction to learners. The components included in the plan are listed in Table 1.1.

Look at Table 1.1 and consider the components that go into an instructional plan. The first component is your *instructional goal*, a general statement of what the learners will be able to do as a result of your instruction. The instructional goal is expressed in a more specific fashion through

TABLE 1.1. Components of an Instructional Plan

A. Instructional goals
B. Objectives for each goal
C. Test items for each objective
D. Instructional activities for each objective or cluster of objectives
   1. Type of instructional activity
   2. Content
   3. Means of presenting instructional activity

a list of *objectives*, explicit statements of what students will be able to do at the end of your instruction. You will modify, as required, your objectives after carefully considering your *students' needs and special characteristics*.

After the objectives have been stated and modified, it is necessary to select or develop *test items* for each of the objectives. Test items enable you to determine whether, in fact, your students have been successful in achieving the objectives. The next component of the overall instructional plan is the list of *instructional activities*, which briefly describes the steps that you will take when you present your students with instruction related to an objective or group of objectives. The description of the activities also includes a listing of the *media*, or means of presentation, you will use.

After you plan for all of the components we have described, you should develop a procedure for linking the components and implementing them in the classroom. In this book we will describe a procedure that you can use to enhance the probability that the students in your class will reach the level of performance you desire for them.

After you implement your instruction, it is important that you examine the performance of your students so that you can ascertain how effective your instruction was. Based upon this information, you can come up with a revised plan for the next time you present the instruction.

To remind you of the interrelationship of the steps to develop effective instruction, we will frequently refer to the accompanying flowchart.

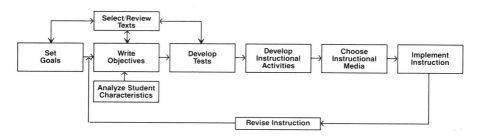

Model for developing effective instruction.

This diagram may look a little complicated at first, but it basically reflects the description of the process that was just discussed. There is one component in the diagram that we omitted from our description: the role of the textbook. When does it come into consideration when instruction is being planned? Ideally, one would develop goals, objectives, and test items before planning instructional activities. In planning the activities, you should consider the textbook to be one of the available means that could be used in teaching specific objectives.

It is more realistic, however, to acknowledge the prominence of the textbook in the instructional planning process. At times it is literally the starting point in the process; so that goals, objectives, tests, and activities are all derived from the content of a textbook that has been selected for a particular course. While we would not advocate this approach, our model indicates that the text can be very influential in the early stages of the planning process. Our discussion of the selection and use of a textbook occurs after consideration of goals, objectives, and tests, and before the development of instructional activities. While this is a relatively arbitrary placement of this chapter, it permits us to use terms and concepts that have been presented earlier in the text.

If the type of instructional plan outlined in Table 1.1 appears rather formidable, we would like to assure you that preparing such a plan is not that difficult, nor is it particularly time-consuming after you have done it several times. Either prior to or during the instructional process, most teachers make decisions about most or all of the components we described. Often, however, those decisions are not made in a systematic fashion. Our goal is to help you to make those decisions systematically. Believe it or not, once you become accustomed to making instructional decisions systematically, you'll find that it won't take you much time to do so! Furthermore, we don't expect that you will be spending every day engaged in this kind of planning. An instructional plan can be used to help prepare a single lesson or an entire unit. You may find that one instructional plan will often help guide you through several weeks of instruction.

The instructional plan does not presuppose any particular approach to teaching. It is based on one fundamental concept: that you are able to state your instructional goals in terms of what you expect your students to do after they have completed your instruction. If you are able to describe the learning outcomes you want your students to attain, then the rest of your plan will flow from those statements. And a great variety of instructional approaches can be employed in order to help your students attain these outcomes. It is important that we stress this flexibility in the planning process we are proposing. As you begin working through the process, please keep in mind that it is not a rigid plan, but rather one that allows for a variety of instructional approaches.

The format we suggest you follow when you describe the various components of your instructional plan should also be viewed as flexible. We believe that it is much more important to systematically plan for each of the components we describe than it is to rigidly adhere to a format for displaying those components. So when you get out there in the "real world of teaching," we will be happy if you engage in the systematic planning process we will be describing, even if your written plan takes a form that is different than the one presented in this book.

TEXT FORMAT

The chapters in this text all have a similar structure. Each has seven major sections. Following a transition statement and a diagram of the planning process, the sections are

- Problem Scenario
- Chapter Objectives
- Background Information
- Major Concepts and Examples
- Practice and Feedback
- Application
- Summary

Problem Scenario

A description of a situation that is all too common in the teaching profession begins each chapter. Each teaching scenario can be addressed by applying the skills described in the chapter, and the situation in the scenario is discussed in later parts of the chapter.

Chapter Objectives

For each chapter there are several major objectives that are stated in terms of what you will be able to do as a result of having read and studied the chapter.

Background Information

This section includes information that helps to bridge the chapter with earlier chapters, and describes related events in the field of education, which should help put the chapter into a larger framework. At times, a theoretical perspective is described.

Major Concepts and Examples

This is the most critical component of each chapter. Major ideas and concepts that apply to the objectives for the chapter are presented here along with examples. In some cases the examples involve descriptions of situations in which the concepts and ideas presented in the chapter are properly applied. In other cases, there are descriptions of improper applications. We point out the major differences between the two!

Practice and Feedback

In each chapter there are a variety of exercises directly related to the objectives of the chapter. After completing these exercises, you will be able to compare your responses with those provided in the feedback section.

Application

As you read this book, it will be most beneficial to develop an instructional plan of your own. The application section of each chapter guides you in developing a specific portion of your plan. By the time you finish this book, you will have developed and evaluated an entire instructional plan.

Summary

This section summarizes the major ideas that have been presented in the chapter and provides a bridge to the succeeding chapter.

SUMMARY

In this chapter we have described effective instruction as instruction that enables students to enjoy their learning of specified skills, knowledge, and attitudes. In order to provide effective instruction, teachers must plan systematically for the activities that will take place in the classroom. An instructional planning model has been presented, which includes as its major components: instructional goals, objectives, test items, and instructional activities. These components are carefully linked and integrated into a strategy which is implemented in the classroom. Data are gathered to evaluate the effectiveness of that instruction for the purpose of revision.

The ideas that are presented in this text have been taken from the field of instructional design. The concepts and procedures are ones that teachers can realistically implement in their classrooms. These procedures are not tied to any particular teaching philosophy. The systematic planning process we describe allows for a variety of instructional approaches. By employing this planning process, you can greatly increase the likelihood that your instruction will be effective.

In the following chapters we will carefully describe each component in the instructional plan. If you would like to get an advanced look at a complete instructional plan, you might examine Chapter Eight, which shows a plan for teaching average students how to solve mathematical word problems.

CHAPTER TWO
SETTING GOALS

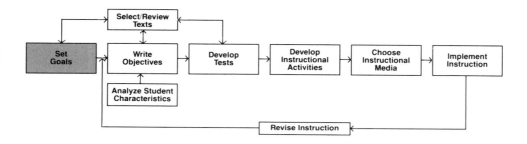

The systematic process for planning instruction always begins with the identification of instructional goals. Where do goals come from, and how are they used? How can goals be categorized and how do they influence instruction? This chapter examines these questions.

PROBLEM SCENARIO

A candidate for school superintendent is addressing a large gathering of parents. The candidate states, "We will strive to have every young person achieve his or her highest potential with regard to intellectual, social, and physical well being." If this person were elected, how could these goals be converted into more specific outcomes for students? What implications are there for the schools' testing and instructional programs?

CHAPTER OBJECTIVES

The objectives for this chapter are that you will be able to

1. describe the sources and instructional uses of goals
2. identify different types of learning outcomes and different levels of intellectual skills

BACKGROUND INFORMATION

We will use goal statements as the entry point for helping you to become a more effective teacher. Without educational goals we are merely carrying out a random set of activities that may or may not be of benefit to learners. The goals we have for our educational programs are the starting points from which we derive all subsequent activities and therefore they are crucial to the teaching/learning process.

Goals are derived from a number of sources and are expressed in a variety of ways. Consider, for example, the following situations that could occur in any school district. We might find administrators arguing the merits of academic skills versus vocational education for students. We might find a group of parents debating, in very loud terms, the pros and cons of introducing a new sex education program in the school district. We might find a group of teachers engaged in a discussion of the merits of a curriculum that stresses the growth and performance of the individual student as opposed to a curriculum that focuses upon the importance of cooperation in groups. And in a specific content area, such as elementary science, we might find the teachers debating the value of students doing experiments against the value of memorizing scientific facts.

Interest in establishing educational goals is not limited to parents, administrators, and teachers. As a result of their concerns for the educational process, state legislators often become involved in the process of goal setting. For example, you might find some legislators advocating that a certain number of hours be spent on writing essays in English classes or that the free enterprise system be stressed in social studies courses.

These situations are representative of the great variety of ways goals are established in the schools. Goal setting is critically important because goals determine, to a large part, what students experience in school and, to some extent, what teachers will actually teach. We will not be discussing a methodology for establishing educational goals. We simply recognize that goals *are* established in a variety of ways and by a variety of sources, and that there is no single or correct set of educational goals. They are continually in transition.

MAJOR CONCEPTS AND EXAMPLES

The goals for our schools are established in many different ways. Some are mandated through legislation. Others are established by accrediting agencies that insist students be able to perform a particular set of skills. Often, the local school board will affirm the goals established by the legislature and accrediting agencies, and then place their own emphasis upon goals they feel are of greatest importance to the local school district.

In every school district there are special interest groups as well as parent/teacher organizations that attempt to influence the interpretation of educational goals and the instruction that is related to them. Similarly, teachers and curriculum supervisors and other administrators influence how the goals are implemented as they attempt to match goals to the curriculum.

Another major source of instructional goals is textbooks. Consider the role of a textbook in any curriculum. It can be argued that, in many teaching situations, the textbook serves as the curriculum. In this case, the goals of the curriculum and the goals expressed in the textbooks are one and the same. At the very least, we know that textbooks often play a major role in influencing what is taught in a course.

The ultimate consumer for any set of goals is the individual teacher. It is the teacher's responsibility to translate the goals into programs for learners and it is the interpretation of, and emphasis on, these goals that determines what is taught in the classroom. Teachers not only affect how goals are implemented; they can also help establish goals. That is, teachers may involve themselves at any of the levels described above to influence the groups that ultimately determine the goals for the curriculum. Therefore, it is important to be aware of both the origins of the goals and the potential range of views that will be held among the people who make up an educational community. Many of these views will ultimately be reflected in the goals of a school district, and will eventually be translated into a curriculum and into instructional and testing processes in the classroom.

Uses of Goals

Goals are often used as the focus for developing a curriculum. For example, a state legislature has mandated that all students in the state must demonstrate mastery of basic skills in mathematics prior to graduating from the eighth grade. Around the state, this goal has not only influenced the content of mathematics programs, but science, home economics, and industrial arts programs as well.

In addition to serving as guides to curriculum development, goals serve a variety of other functions. For example, they can be used to inform the public of what a school or school district is trying to achieve. Goal statements such as "each student will have mastered basic mathematical skills prior to graduation from eighth grade" describe a school's priorities; such statements help the public determine the instructional emphasis in a school. A set of goal statements for a school district may also be used to determine the consistency of those goals with state mandates and guidelines set forth by accrediting agencies.

Goals also provide guidance for testing programs in schools. If schools are to be accountable for their goals, they must determine if their goals are being achieved. To do this, a testing program must be established which directly measures attainment of the established goals. In the example of a goal related to basic skills in mathematics, there must be a basic skills test in mathematics administered to all eighth grade students to determine if they have mastered these skills. In some states, both the goals and the corresponding tests are developed at the state level and provided to the districts for their use.

In the final analysis, the identification of goals provides direction for the instructional activities that take place in the classroom. Let's take a closer look at these goals.

Characteristics of Goals

Goal statements vary a great deal. They certainly differ in terms of how general or specific they are, ranging from ones that are so vague that you would find it almost impossible to know how to implement them, to ones that are extremely detailed. Goals may also differ in terms of their focus of action. For example, some describe what a school will achieve, while others focus on what teachers will do, and still others describe what will be expected of students. The goals that will be of greatest importance to us are those that specify the types of learning students should achieve or the kinds of *student behaviors* that we would like to see.

In the scenario at the beginning of this chapter, a candidate for school superintendent talked about student-oriented goals, stating that educational goals should include the enhancement of students' intellectual, social, and physical behavior. The three types of behaviors the candidate referred to are very different from one another. Not only are they different in terms of how they are performed, they are also quite different in terms of how they should be taught. In other words, the instructional activities you use to teach your students a physical behavior (also known as a motor skill) is quite different from the activities used to teach an intellectual skill. Because the activities you use differ depending upon the type of behavior (or learning outcome) you want your students to acquire, you must be able to differentiate among various types of learning outcomes.

Classification of Learning Outcomes

Learning outcomes can refer either to goals, or to more specific objectives derived from the goals. In either case, learning outcomes are descriptions of what students should be able to do as a result of instruction. There are four different types, or domains, of learning outcomes. These domains are

- Knowledge
- Intellectual skills
- Motor skills
- Attitudes

Knowledge Learning outcomes in the domain we call "knowledge" deal directly with student ability to recall and remember specific information. It's the kind of learning required of students when we ask them to learn the capitals of the states, the names of the presidents, or the symbols for the chemical elements. We usually refer to these sorts of tasks as memorization and, in some settings, a great deal of instruction is directed toward facilitating memorization of specific information.

Intellectual skills Intellectual skills are those processes used by students that go above and beyond the pure memorization of information to the actual use of the information. Almost every course in the public school curriculum emphasizes, to a greater or lesser extent, a variety of intellectual skills that students must learn. Just as intellectual skills are different from motor skills or knowledge, there are also different levels of these intellectual skills. It is important to be aware of these levels.

The lowest level of intellectual skill is that of *concept learning*. In simple terms, a concept is a label used to describe a group of related things or ideas. When we say that a student "understands" or has learned a concept, we mean that he or she is able to identify correctly whether a particular thing or idea can be classified as an example of that concept. For example, if a student "understands" the concept of a chair, he or she should be able to indicate whether or not a particular item is a chair.

The ability to understand various concepts is an important intellectual skill. Teachers spend a great deal of time teaching young children about concepts such as color, democracy, space, and so on. The importance of learning about concepts is not limited, however, to elementary school children. At the high school level, we get involved in teaching students about more complex concepts, such as electrons and ions. The task for the student is to use the parameters of what constitutes an electron to determine if particular examples are, in fact, electrons.

A second, and higher, level of intellectual skills is *rule using*. Rules are combinations of concepts. For example, the Pythagorean theorem states that "the length of the hypotenuse of a right triangle equals the square root of the sum of the squares of the length of the other two sides." In order to use this rule, learners must understand each of the concepts that are part of it, such as what is meant by square root, hypotenuse, and right triangle. Simply stating or writing the theorem is not an example of rule using. That is knowledge. The rule must actually be applied and the result determined in order to say that a student is using a rule.

The third and highest level of intellectual skills is *problem solving*. As in the case of rule using, when students engage in problem solving, they apply rules to help them solve problems. The distinction between problem solving and rule using is that in rule using, the student is asked to correctly use a given rule, whereas in problem solving, the student is given a problem to solve and must choose and correctly use the appropriate rules to solve the problem. In the former case, the student may be asked to use the Pythagorean theorem to determine the length of the side of a triangle, while in the latter the student may be asked to generate a solution to the problem of what to do with our garbage.

Motor skills Any physical activity that requires movement of all or part of the body is referred to as a motor skill. We are not referring to acts such as pushing a button, but rather more complex physical activities such as those involved in dancing, creating crafts, operating a sewing machine, or throwing a football. Motor skills can be learned in the context of individual activities or team activities, and are an important part of the public school curriculum.

Attitudes The personal feelings and beliefs that result in a person's tendency to act in a particular way are referred to as attitudes. We often refer to someone's attitude about some topic or activity such as the environment; when we do so, we are usually referring to their general tendency to respond in a particular way with regard to the environment. One of the major goals of education is to shape the attitudes of the learners so that they will make responsible choices throughout their lives.

Let's look at the four major types of learning outcomes and an example of each.

EXAMPLES OF TYPES OF LEARNING OUTCOMES

Type of Learning Outcome	Sample Goal
Knowledge	Recite the Gettysburg Address
Intellectual skill	Classify various types of chemical reactions
Motor skill	Improve ability to skip rope
Attitude	Choose to share

Now that we have indicated how goals can be classified in four broad categories, consider this one: Able to use a recipe to bake a cake from scratch for a given number of people. This goal, and others like it, begins to present us with some problems when we try to classify it into one of the four major domains. Some of the steps in baking a cake involve motor skills (for example, breaking the eggs and stirring the batter). However, other steps involve intellectual skills (for example, computing the right amount of each ingredient for cakes of different sizes). The point here is that many important goals, and particularly those dealing with attitudes, contain skills from more than one domain. This will become more apparent as we consider how to develop instructional activities for a goal that has multiple learning outcomes.

Specificity of Instructional Goals

If you review the various examples of goals that we have used in this chapter, you will find that they vary greatly in their specificity. While they all focus on what students will be able to do, some are so general that we would have to break them down into much more specific behaviors before we could think about how we would prepare to teach them. Others are sufficiently specific that we could imagine a one-hour lesson that would be more than sufficient for students to achieve the goal. There is no standard unit for determining the "size" of a goal. We have to accept this ambiguity at this point in the planning process, with the understanding that later on we will have to become more specific about student learning outcomes if we have started with fairly general goals.

The School Superintendent's Campaign Promise

Let's step back and consider what has been said in this chapter and the implications of the campaign promise made by the candidate for the superintendent's position. First we have indicated that instructional goals represent what students will be able to do following instruction. Some goals or outcomes are representative of knowledge, while others are intellectual skills, motor skills, or attitudes. In addition, among intellectual skills we can differentiate among concepts, rules, and problem solving. The importance of these distinctions will become very clear as we move through the process of establishing an instructional plan. Depending on the domain of the learning outcome, we will use quite different approaches to the instructional process.

In light of the importance of goals, the candidate's emphasis on "intellectual, social and physical well being" is about as general as goal statements can be. In order to identify more specific kinds of student behaviors that would be representative of these goals, it would be necessary to consult the various sources of the goals described in this chapter. These more specific student behaviors would, in turn, influence the instructional and testing programs in the school.

PRACTICE

Listed below are five sets of questions. After you have answered the questions, compare your answers with the suggested answers in the feedback section that follows.

1. Describe four important sources of educational goals. Indicate which source you believe is most important.
2. From the standpoint of instructional planning, what is the most important use of educational goals?

3. Listed below are a number of possible educational goals. Indicate which ones are described in terms of student behaviors.
    A. All students will be treated alike.
    B. Students will be able to write effectively.
    C. Students will have an outstanding school.
    D. Students will be able to engage in good health habits.
    E. Promote student loyalty to the community.

4. Listed below are a number of educational goals. Classify each into one of the following domains: knowledge, intellectual skill, motor skill, or attitude.
    A. Students will be able to operate an electric saw.
    B. Students will choose to demonstrate courteous behavior in the halls.
    C. Students will be able to list the titles of five of Shakespeare's plays.
    D. Students will be able to classify examples of seashells into three major categories.
    E. Students will be able to propose a strategy for caring for the homeless.

5. Listed below are three intellectual skills. Classify these skills as concept learning, rule using or problem solving.
    A. Students will be able to place commas at appropriate places in a paragraph.
    B. Students will be able to identify verbs in sentences.
    C. Students will be able to edit a poorly written paragraph.

FEEDBACK

1. There are many sources of educational goals, and it is very difficult to single out one as being the most important. Perhaps you mentioned *parents*. Parents certainly are an important source of goals, but the way they influence goals is often through their *school boards, school administrators*, and *state legislatures*. State legislatures establish the mandatory goals for schools, while local school boards provide their own interpretation and add a local dimension to those goals. And, of course, *teachers* play an important role in the goal-setting process, primarily in terms of determining which goals will be emphasized in the classroom. You may have also noted that the *textbook* which is chosen for a course may become a source for goal statements. In addition to these sources, *accrediting agencies*, and *special interest groups* also have an important influence on the setting of educational goals.

2. Although statements of goals serve many purposes in communicating to the community what it is schools are attempting to accomplish, for our purposes the most important function goals serve is that they are the starting point for determining what and, to a certain extent, how content will be taught in the classroom.

3. The goals stated in terms of student behaviors are (b), "all students will be able to write effectively" and (d), "students will be able to engage in good health habits." The other three alternatives do not directly involve student behavior. Choice (a), "all students will be treated alike," is not a student learning outcome. It appears to be a description of how teachers are to treat students. Choice (c), "students will have an outstanding school," is certainly important, but it's too vague a statement to serve as a goal from which instructional practices could be derived. Alternative (e), "promote student loyalty to

the community," describes a goal for the school, but doesn't really indicate how the students would display that loyalty to the community.

4. The five skills should be classified as follows: (a) motor skill, (b) attitude, (c) knowledge, (d) intellectual skill (concept), and (e) intellectual skill (problem solving).

5. The three types of intellectual skills are: (a) rules, (b) concepts, and (c) problem solving.

APPLICATION

The application section of each chapter includes suggestions for a project that you might undertake. The project is one that you will work on as you proceed through this book. It will begin with the identification of a set of goals and proceed through the planning of an actual lesson which will be implemented in a classroom and revised. In each subsequent chapter you will learn how to do a part of the lesson planning process.

To begin the project, write several goals related to your own area of interest and expertise. If you do not feel confident about using a particular academic content area, consider a special hobby or interest that you have that others might want to learn about. Identify at least one goal for each of the four major domains of learning outcomes described in this chapter. These goals should focus on what students will be able to do, and not on what a teacher or school will be attempting to accomplish.

The goals you prepare for this assignment will serve as the basis for additional activities you will conduct in subsequent chapters. Choose your goals carefully and make sure that they are in areas in which you have sufficient knowledge to develop instruction.

SUMMARY

In the field of education, goals are derived from a variety of sources and serve a variety of purposes. For the purpose of instructional planning, the most important goals are those that are described in terms of actual student learning outcomes, that is, goals that describe behaviors and attitudes that students should exhibit when they complete their instruction.

There are four major domains of learning outcomes: knowledge, intellectual skills, motor skills, and attitudes. Being able to distinguish among these domains will become important when you develop instructional activities to help your students achieve your instructional goals. Regardless of the sources or the type of learning outcomes they represent, goals serve as the starting point for planning instruction. Goals are the basis for identifying the specific objectives for your instruction. The topic of the next chapter is how to develop those objectives.

CHAPTER THREE
WRITING OBJECTIVES

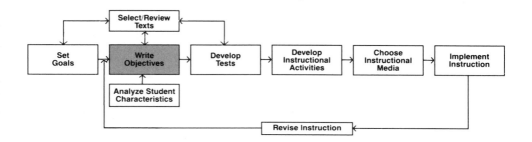

A school's instructional goals directly influence the objectives that are to be achieved by students. The objectives indicate more specifically what students should be able to do as a result of the instruction they receive.

PROBLEM SCENARIO

The teachers in the English department in a local high school are examining the school district's goals in their area with the intent of translating those goals into specific instructional objectives for learners. They have just encountered the following goal: Students will be able to write effectively.

A lively discussion has taken place. What does it mean to write effectively? Does it mean that all of the students can write an essay? If so, how good must that essay be? Would being able to write a simple note that conveys information accurately be sufficient? How will students demonstrate that they have effectively achieved this goal? How do we get from very general goals to statements of specific skills that students must achieve?

CHAPTER OBJECTIVES

The objectives for this chapter are that you will be able to

1. identify objectives that are written in correct three-component form
2. describe how objectives may be used
3. write objectives for various types of instructional goals

BACKGROUND INFORMATION

People have advocated the use of objectives in education for many years. Perhaps the person who is best known in this regard is Robert Mager, who popularized the notion of behavioral objectives. Mager's point of view was that to teach, we had to know exactly what the students would be able to do when they completed our instruction. He argued that before we ever begin to develop instruction, we must state our objectives in terms of student outcomes. These objectives then guide the rest of the instructional process.

This emphasis on the development of objectives became very controversial. There were those who strongly endorsed Mager's efforts to clearly specify those things that were to be learned by students. However, there were others who said that the use of behavioral objectives was very detrimental. They argued that because we only stated very specific observable behaviors in objectives, we often ended up only writing objectives about the most trivial outcomes of education. Furthermore, critics felt that things inside the learner which we couldn't see were the important changes that were taking place. In addition, they argued that the behavioral objectives essentially dictated the curriculum and the things teachers could do at any given time. Objectives, they said, removed the possibility of taking advantage of "teachable moments" in the classroom, those moments that would spontaneously arise and provide teachers with an opportunity to teach students something that was possibly outside the range of the normal curriculum. Critics of objectives argued that if teachers strictly adhered to teaching by objectives, they would ignore those "teachable moments."

Although many of these types of arguments and beliefs concerning behavioral objectives exist to this day, an increasing number of teachers are finding objectives to be useful. Teachers realize that objectives can guide and increase the effectiveness of the instructional process and serve as a means of communicating to students, parents, administrators, and other educators what it is that they are trying to achieve in the classroom. Many teachers now realize that objectives do not necessarily limit the instructional methods they use or prevent them from capitalizing upon "teachable moments." Instead, objectives help teachers to focus upon the outcomes of instruction and enable them to recognize whether their students have attained those outcomes.

MAJOR CONCEPTS AND EXAMPLES

Descriptions of what students are expected to do as a result of instruction have been variously labeled "behavioral objectives," "performance objectives," and "instructional objectives." An objective must express in a clear fashion some observable behavior that students are expected to perform or achieve. Therefore, you should write objectives using such verbs as *explain, list, climb, spell, rotate*, and so on. These verbs are often referred to as action verbs, and describe an observable action in which a learner will engage, or an action that will result in an observable product, such as an essay or a list of names.

Conversely, you should not write objectives that include such verbs as *know, understand*, or *appreciate*. These verbs, and others like them, do not describe observable behaviors. Instead they describe internal mental states that mean different things to different people. For example, how can you tell whether a student "knows" the concept "democracy?" Does the student know the concept if the student can define what the term "democracy" means? How about if the student can name several countries that have democratic forms of government? Or perhaps the student should be able to tell us whether a particular form of government we describe is a democracy. If our objective is that a student "knows" the concept of democracy, it is important that we are clear about which behavior we want the student to exhibit.

We do not want you to get the impression that we think that mental processes like thinking and appreciating are unimportant. Quite the contrary! These are the essence of education. We, as teachers, must help students effectively process information and become effective problem solvers. However, the only way we can observe how effective we have been is by observing and assessing the results of the use of these processes. The only way we can tell whether a student knows, understands, or appreciates something is to have the student *do something* to demonstrate that knowledge, understanding, or appreciation. It is that "something" (be it defining a term, identifying examples of a term, or something else), which we need to specify in a behavioral objective.

Components of an Objective

An objective consists of three basic components. The first describes the actual *behavior* we expect our students to exhibit as a result of instruction. Examples of such behaviors would include writing the names of the capitals of various states, determining the answers to various multiplication problems, identifying examples of reptiles, setting up a television camera, and choosing to throw trash in a litter basket rather than on the ground.

The second component of an objective is a description of the *conditions* under which the student will be required to exhibit the desired behavior. For example, if students are expected to describe the strengths and weaknesses of Article I of the Constitution, will they be required to recall, from memory, the provisions of that Article, or will they be allowed to refer to a copy of Article I as they attempt to describe its strengths and weaknesses? In the first case, the conditions would be stated: "without any reference materials, the student will . . ." In the latter case, the conditions would be: "Given a copy of Article I of the Constitution, the student will . . ."

If students must draw a circle, will they be able to use a compass or must they draw it free hand? In solving a number of numerical problems, will students be able to use their calculators or will they be required to do their own computations? Each of these questions focuses upon what will be available to students when they are performing the behavior described in an objective. In other words, the questions focus upon the conditions under which a behavior will be performed. By asking yourself, "what will be available to students at the time I assess their performance?" you will be able to identify the conditions portion of your objectives.

It is important to note that the conditions portion of an objective does not include statements like "after listening to my instructions" or "after going through the workbook" or "after studying the reading package." An objective does not state how the learner will acquire a new skill or knowledge, it simply indicates the conditions under which it will be performed after it has been taught.

The third and final component of an objective is referred to as the *criterion*, or *standard* which must be met in order for the performance to be judged acceptable. Perhaps the standard you are most familiar with is that a test score of 90 percent and above is an A, 80 through 89 percent is a B, and so on. This standard indicates, in a very general way, the level of performance a student must attain in order to receive a particular grade.

The standards described in an objective are specific to the behavior described in that objective. For example, an objective might indicate that the student must correctly solve three out of four problems, or must correctly list four out of five titles. Other examples of standards would be that a student would make no more than three errors while performing a procedure, or that a student would choose a particular course of action in at least two out of three opportunities. It is assumed that the teacher writing an objective has sufficient knowledge of the content to specify the criterion students must meet to master the objective.

In addition to describing how well a student will be expected to perform a behavior, a standard may describe how quickly the student will be expected to perform it. For example, a standard may indicate that a student must be able to perform a certain skill, such as solving a physics problem, within a period of ten minutes.

Sample Objectives

Now let's examine some objectives to determine their strengths and weaknesses. For example, consider this objective: "Without the use of any materials, the student will be able to list the titles of five Shakespearean plays. All five titles must be exactly correct." The first thing we will note about this objective is that it falls in the domain of knowledge because it requires the student to recall some information. We are asking the student to retrieve from memory the names of five Shakespearean plays.

You should note several other things about this objective. The first is that students are to perform this objective "without the use of any materials." Secondly, note that the objective actually contains two sentences. The standard, that all the titles must be exactly correct, is stated in a separate sentence. This is perfectly appropriate. Sometimes an objective can be communicated more clearly by breaking it into two or three sentences.

Here is a motor skill objective: "With a partner in a kneeling position, the student will execute the takedown hold according to the procedure described in the wrestling textbook." This is an objective in which the criterion for performance depends, in part, upon the instructor's judgment. It is clear that the student is to execute a particular wrestling hold from a starting position as described in the text, but how will the instructor judge whether the hold has been properly executed? At the very least, the instructor should have a checklist of the steps that should be performed when executing a takedown hold. The checklist could be in his head or, better yet, the instructor could prepare a brief written checklist to judge whether each student had executed the takedown hold properly. It is usually wise to develop a brief checklist of the sequence of steps to properly execute any motor skill. By using such a checklist, an instructor may be better able to judge objectively whether a particular motor skill has been performed properly.

Let's look at another type of objective: "Given the opportunity to cheat by copying from another student, the student will choose not to cheat 100 percent of the time." We can see the three components of the objective here: "given the opportunity to cheat by copying from another student" would be the conditions; "choose not to cheat" would be the behavior; and the standard is "100 percent of the time." Although this objective includes the three major components, we would have difficulty in determining whether our students consistently behave in this fashion outside the classroom. At best, perhaps we can judge whether a student fails to achieve the objective by observing the cheating that takes place in the classroom. The general point to be made here is that while your goals can focus on behaviors that take place outside the classroom, most of your objectives should focus on behaviors you can observe while your students are in school.

Now let's turn to what we consider to be the "universal objective." It's universal because it covers almost all behaviors at all times, but says absolutely nothing. Consider this objective: "Given a multiple choice test, the student will circle the correct answer to nine of ten questions." This objective certainly contains a set of conditions, namely, "given a multiple choice test." The behavior is to circle the answers, and the standard is to answer nine of ten questions correctly. We have an objective that meets all of the criteria for an objective, but the objective describes absolutely nothing about the content or substance of the real behavior we are interested in. When you write your objectives, be careful that you describe the content of the behavior you want to see and don't fall into the trap of writing a "universal objective."

It may be helpful to review some verbs that can be used to describe student behavior in the various domains of learning outcomes that we have already discussed. If you have an objective in the knowledge domain, then the behavior you are asking a student to perform basically is to *list* or *state* or to *describe* something from memory; or, perhaps, to *recognize* items from a list of things that the student has learned before.

If your objective is in the intellectual skills domain, then in all likelihood you are asking students to demonstrate their knowledge of concepts, rules, or problem solving strategies. The corresponding verbs for these types of behaviors are to *classify* (concepts), to *apply* (rules), and to *solve* (problems).

In the motor skill domain you are nearly always asking students to either *perform* or *execute* some routine which they have already learned.

In the attitude domain we always use the word *choose* because we are asking students to reflect their feelings and beliefs by choosing a particular behavior to be exhibited. Here we are using the word *choose* not in the multiple-choice sense of that word, as when a student must choose the correct answer, but rather in terms of choosing some behavior from an array of possible behaviors. It is assumed that choosing a behavior that is appropriate for a particular setting reflects the student's real feelings and beliefs about that setting.

SUGGESTED VERBS FOR INSTRUCTIONAL OBJECTIVES

Domain of the Objective	Suggested Verbs
Knowledge	List, state, describe, recognize
Intellectual Skills	Classify, apply, solve
Motor Skills	Perform, execute
Attitudes	Choose

Listed above are the verbs we suggest you use. You may find these verbs helpful as you write objectives for goals that you have identified. However, do not feel that only these verbs can be used to develop an acceptable objective. These are only suggestions. It is more important to state objectives in a way which is meaningful to you, and subsequently meaningful to learners, than it is to state objectives in a more stylized fashion which does not, in fact, represent what you mean.

Deriving Objectives from Goals

How do we get from goal statements to specific objectives? If you look in a textbook, you may find that the authors have stated rather broad general goals followed by specific objectives. That is the same kind of process that you will have to go through if objectives are not readily available to you. However, even if objectives are available to you, you should check to see if they are representative of a particular goal your students are expected to attain. Let's look at an example of how you might go about this process.

Let us say that we have the goal: "The students will develop appropriate life-long health habits." We could convert that into many specific objectives. Some of those objectives might be things such as "being able to list the major bones in the leg," "being able to demonstrate appropriate techniques for brushing teeth," "being able to appropriately diagnose when to go to a doctor," and "choosing to use drugs appropriately." Are the behaviors described in these objectives representative of our goal?

Before we answer the question we have raised, note two things about the objectives that have been described here. First of all, they are written in brief form and are not complete objectives. Second, note that each of the four objectives represents a different domain of learning outcome. Thus we have an example of a goal that has resulted in objectives in the four different domains. As noted earlier, this is not unusual. A good way to derive objectives from a goal would be to think of appropriate objectives in each domain.

Now let's examine whether the objectives we identified are appropriate in light of our goal. In order to develop appropriate life-long health habits, is it really important for our students to be "able to list the major bones in the leg "? Probably not, and therefore we probably should delete this objective because it is unrelated to our goal of developing appropriate life-long health habits.

The other three objectives we identified in relation to our goal seem to be more appropriate. Choosing a drug-free lifestyle and being able to correctly determine when to go to the doctor certainly seem like behaviors related to developing good life-long health habits. Being able to brush one's own teeth properly also is important, but you might question whether that is a behavior that should be assessed in school. That point is certainly debatable, and the answer depends, in part, on the age and mental capabilities of the learners.

The teachers in the English department who were described in the problem scenario at the beginning of this chapter would have to go through a similar process to identify specific objectives for the goal of writing effectively. In this particular example, it is possible to generate a wide range of intellectual skills objectives. It would also be important to consider any attitudes that should be developed with regard to writing. After the objectives have been generated it would be important to compare them with lists of state and district competencies, and objectives in popular texts. With this information, plus information about the skills and attitudes of the students, it would be necessary to reduce the list to those which are of greatest importance and relevance to the students. This may require a long, but important, dialogue among teachers.

What we have done in this section is provide an example of how you might determine if a series of objectives is appropriate for a given goal. If you use a procedure like the one we described, and you find that an objective does not seem to be related to a particular goal, then you may want to consider eliminating that objective from your curriculum, if you have that option.

Value of Objectives

The instructional goal we referred to in the last section was that students would develop appropriate life-long health habits. Developing instructional activities for a goal such as this, or nearly any goal, is difficult. Goals, by their very nature, are usually broad and general, and sometimes rather vague. Objectives, however, are more specific and therefore serve as a better basis for planning instructional activities. In later chapters we will show you how to use your objectives as the basis for planning the instruction you will present to your students.

While objectives serve to describe what students will be able to do when they finish some instruction, and to guide the planning of instruction, they also serve a number of other useful purposes. Teachers can, and should, use objectives to help them design tests. We will talk about using objectives for this purpose in Chapter Five. Teachers can share their objectives with their students to let them know what they will be expected to learn. In addition, objectives are very valuable for administrators because they have to relate the school curriculum to state and district standards, and they have to communicate with others about their curriculum. Finally, objectives are very useful when talking with parents about what students are learning.

Short Forms of Objectives

Have you noticed that the objectives which are stated for our chapters are not complete, three-component objectives? We often omit the conditions and the criteria from our objectives and simply state the behaviors that we expect you to learn.

This manner of describing the objectives was a deliberate decision on our part, and was done to communicate to you, the learner, the importance of the behaviors we hope to teach. It is a good idea to write all three components of an objective when you are planning your instructional activities and designing your tests. However, it is often easier to communicate your objectives to others (particularly your students) by dropping either the conditions or the standards from your objectives and simply describing the behaviors you would like to see attained.

Let's look at objectives in the four domains and see to what extent they might be shortened in order to simplify the communication of the behaviors in the objectives. In the knowledge domain, it is usually important to state the conditions under which the behavior will be demonstrated. We need to know whether students will be able to use aids to help them recall information or whether the information must be memorized. The exact standard that students must meet when they are recalling information is often not necessary, however. Therefore, when you are communicating knowledge objectives to your students, a statement of the behavior and conditions will often suffice.

For intellectual skills, the conditions under which the skill will be demonstrated often are implied. For example, being able to multiply whole numbers implies that the student will be given a set of whole-number multiplication problems. Thus, stating that the students will be given these problems is unnecessary. If, however, students will be allowed to use a calculator to solve the problems, this should be indicated. As was the case with knowledge objectives, it often seems unnecessary to include your standards. For intellectual skills objectives, you may choose to provide only a statement of the behavior in which you are interested.

For motor skills, the conditions are often implied, but it is usually important to describe the standard against which a skill will be judged. By providing your students with standards, you will give them an indication of the precision and speed with which you expect them to perform a motor skill.

In the attitude domain, you will usually be asking your students to choose to act in a particular manner under a given set of circumstances. Thus, often it is necessary to indicate the conditions under which that choice will have to be made. It seems less important, however, to describe the standard you will use to judge your students' attainment of objectives in this domain, other than to hope that the behavior does occur and get reinforced.

SHORT FORMS OF OBJECTIVES

Domain	Components Usually Included
Knowledge	Conditions, Behavior
Intellectual Skills	Behavior
Motor Skills	Behavior, Standard
Attitudes	Conditions, Behavior

Discussing the short form of objectives is not common. Most references stick very closely to the concept of a three-component objective, namely conditions, behavior, and standard. However, we believe you must be flexible when you use objectives. If communication can be improved by making an objective less cumbersome, we think you should do so. This is no substitute, however, for knowing what you want students to be able to do. For the purposes of planning instruction and designing tests, all three components of an objective should be explicit and well understood. However, when that same objective is being described to others, the various short forms described above may be used to facilitate communication.

PRACTICE

1. Listed below are seven objectives. Read each of the objectives and determine if it is a complete three-component objective. If not, indicate what is missing and correct the objective.

A. Given a lathe, the student will operate it by making a round post out of a square block.

B. Without any aid, identify the major crops raised in the southeastern United States by selecting the four correct items from a list of seven.

C. The student will choose not to bump into other students who pass him or her in a hallway.

D. Given fifteen colored blocks, the student will be able to classify them correctly on the basis of their color.

E. Given a poorly written paragraph, the student will edit it and correct 90 percent of the errors.

F. The student will know all about photosynthesis.

G. Without the use of any aids, the student will be able to match at least eight items correctly.

2. Listed below are three possible goals that might be established by a school district. For each goal, list at least one objective.

A. Be a good citizen.

B. Be a learner throughout life.

C. Know the basic skills of arithmetic.

3. Listed below are four objectives. Indicate how, if at all, you would modify these objectives for the following two purposes. First, if you were to inform your students what they were going to learn in your class, and second, if you were to tell parents at an open house what their children were learning in your class.

A. With the aid of the text, the student can correctly list at least four causes of the Civil War.

B. Given a standard baseball field, the student can throw from home plate to first base so that the ball can be caught by a person at first base four out of five times.

C. Given a choice of attending or not attending, the student will choose to go to a symphony concert at least one out of two times.

D. Given a list of ten vocabulary words, the student will correctly read eight.

4. Mr. Smith is preparing a test on the Civil War, but is not sure what should be on his test. As we stated earlier, objectives serve many purposes. How could objectives be helpful to Mr. Smith?

FEEDBACK

1. A. This objective is complete because the conditions and the behavior are specified along with a qualitative description of the criterion. However, if the speed with which this task is done is of importance, then a criterion involving time, such as "within fifteen minutes," should have been added to the objective.

B. This objective clearly specifies a behavior (identify), conditions (without any aid), and standard (selecting the correct four from the list of seven). The objective is properly written.

C. This objective, dealing with bumping into students in the hall is complete. While it seems to be rather vague, it reflects the kinds of problems we have when we start writing attitudinal objectives. As an alternative, we could say, "In a crowded hallway, the student will let other students pass by without bumping them." Here the criterion would be "without bumping them" and the condition would be "in a crowded hallway."

D. This is a complete objective. Any time a word like "correctly" appears in an objective, we have to assume that 100 percent correct performance is desired. In this case, unless we wanted the student to classify blocks with 100 percent accuracy, a criterion like "twelve out of fifteen" would have to be stated.

E. This objective dealing with proofreading a paragraph and finding and correcting the errors is appropriately written.

F. We hope that you found this to be a very unsatisfactory objective. "Knowing all about photosynthesis" is not an acceptable objective for a number of reasons. First of all, we really don't know what the behavior is; we don't know what "knowing" really means. It might mean describing the process, or correctly ordering the steps in the process. In addition, it is unclear as to the conditions under which the students would indicate what they know about photosynthesis. It is also unclear as to how well they would have to know it. If we knew all of these things, we would have a much better statement of the objective. The objective might be "Without any aid, the student will describe photosynthesis as the process which plants use to convert the sun's energy into food." In this case, the criterion is an actual description of the words that the student should approximate in his or her answer.

G. We hope you recognized this objective as a form of the "universal objective." It has all three components, but can you tell what the student will really know or be able to do after completing the objective?

2. You were asked to develop objectives for each of the goals that were listed. There is an infinite array of objectives which might have been listed, but let us give you some examples.

A. For the goal "Be a good citizen," you might have stated something like "Given a situation in which an election of a class officer is to be held, the student will always choose to cast a vote."

B. For the goal "Be a learner throughout life," you might have written an objective like "Given a situation in which there is no teacher, the student can describe how to go about learning a new topic." Or you might be more specific by saying "Given fifteen minutes in the school library, the student will be able to locate at least two books on a topic that will be assigned to him or her."

C. For the goal "Know the basic skills of arithmetic," you might have an objective such as "Without any aid, the student will be able to solve fifty single-digit addition problems within two minutes."

Your objectives might be quite different from the ones we have listed. However, make sure that each contains the specific behaviors that could be observed, the conditions under which those behaviors occur, and the standards that can be used to judge whether the behavior is performed in a satisfactory manner.

3. You were presented with four objectives and asked how you would modify those objectives if you were going to communicate them to students and to parents. You might argue that in each case it is important to be very explicit when communicating with students and therefore they are entitled to see the entire objective as it was listed. However, you might argue that the conditions associated with each of the objectives are not that critical, or are implied. For example, in the case of the baseball throwing objective, it might not be necessary to indicate that the behavior will be done on a "standard baseball field."

What do you think should be said to the parents? In communicating with them, you might drop both the conditions and the criteria. That is, what you want the parents to know is that the students are learning about the Civil War, or learning to throw a baseball, or learning to read vocabulary words, or learning to appreciate symphony music. It may not be necessary to be any more specific with parents than that, unless there is a specific problem with a student. Then more details might be helpful.

4. You were asked to describe how Mr. Smith might use objectives to help him prepare a test on the Civil War. We hope that you said that if Mr. Smith had some specific objectives describing the skills or knowledge he wanted his students to acquire about the Civil War, then he could develop a test that reflected the behaviors described in those objectives. For example, if one of his objectives was to have students identify the sites of the major battles of the Civil War, then that would certainly have to be one of the questions on the test. If another of his objectives involved a higher-level problem-solving skill, such as "The student will describe his or her interpretation of the probable consequences if the South had won the Civil War," then an essay question asking the student to do this should appear on the test. Using instructional objectives to help design tests is a topic we will discuss in greater detail in Chapter Five.

APPLICATION

In the previous chapter, as part of the application activities, you wrote at least one goal for each of the four major domains of learning outcomes. Now you should write one or more objectives for each of those goals. Write each objective as though you were going to use it for instructional planning purposes. That is, make sure that it is a three-component objective that describes a specific behavior, conditions, and criteria.

SUMMARY

In this chapter we have described how objectives are derived from, and are detailed statements of, educational goals. Objectives clearly express what students will be able to do as a result of instruction. Objectives never describe what teachers will be doing.

The three basic components of any objective are the *behavior* expected of the student, the *conditions* under which this behavior will be demonstrated, and the *standard*, or *criterion*, which must be reached by the student. When objectives are used for planning instruction, all three components should be in place. However, when communicating with parents, students, or the community, it be beneficial to shorten the objectives to emphasize the behaviors that are to be learned.

CHAPTER FOUR
ANALYZING STUDENT CHARACTERISTICS

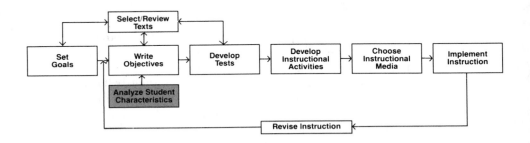

Initially, objectives are written to reflect the desired outcomes of instruction as represented by our educational goals. However, it is sometimes necessary to modify objectives because of the knowledge and skills of the students who will receive the instruction. In this chapter we will examine the modification of objectives on the basis of important student characteristics.

PROBLEM SCENARIO

Ms. Helmer has worked hard at developing a presentation for her low-ability students on how to compute percentages. The state has mandated this as a skill for all the students at the eighth-grade level. In her introductory lesson, Ms. Helmer defined what a percentage is and then used the blackboard to show the students how to solve a number of percentage problems. However, she found that the students were puzzled and unable to answer her questions about the procedures for computing percentages. When she passed out a worksheet, almost none of the students were able to begin solving the problems. Clearly, Ms. Helmer and the students have a problem. What would you suggest with regard to the objective the students are trying to achieve?

CHAPTER OBJECTIVES

The objectives for this chapter are that you will be able to

1. describe the importance of determining students' prerequisite skills, knowledge and attitudes
2. describe how instructional objectives may be modified on the basis of students' skills, knowledge, and attitudes

BACKGROUND INFORMATION

We have stated that systematic planning of instruction starts with goals. Often, however, goals are rather general statements that are not very well defined. We have indicated that these goals must be made more specific, and that this can be done by writing objectives which describe student behaviors. These objectives are stated in such a way that we assume that all students will be able to achieve them. However, it is clear that in any school there is a wide range of differences among students in various classes; and even within classes, large individual differences among the students are likely to exist. Recognition of these differences will be important in determining whether your instructional plan will be a success or a failure.

In this text, we will be considering students who are grouped into three major categories. Those categories are often labeled above average, average, and below average, or learning disabled. Like any labels, these categories mask many differences within the groups, and often children placed in one group might be better served by being in another group. However, schools frequently place students within these categories on the basis of IQ tests. For example, students with IQ's of 130 or above are often considered above average, if not gifted, and those in the IQ range of eighty to ninety-five are considered handicapped or learning disabled. We do not consider these labels to be very important, but we do think it is important that you think about the actual differences among students as you develop your instructional objectives and subsequent plans.

Consider the following question: Will you be teaching students or will you be teaching content? In this question we are referring to a dilemma that often perplexes teachers. On the one hand, teachers are confronted with a set of state or local competencies that are to be achieved by *all* their students; on the other hand, not all the students in a teacher's class are alike; the students in a particular class may vary greatly in terms of their learning abilities.

It is apparent that at times a teacher will be forced to take the attitude that he or she will teach content, and those students who are capable of learning the content will do so and others will simply not be able to. Nonetheless, the teacher will have covered the content as outlined in the text or stated in the district set of competencies.

There will be other times, however, when a teacher may simply decide that it is not possible for the students who are in the class to master all the content that is supposed to be covered. Therefore, the teacher may proceed to make adjustments to the objectives for the class in order to bring the objectives into alignment with the capabilities of the students.

There is no one best answer to this dilemma. We would all like to find ourselves in a situation in which we are able to successfully teach all the content—the skills, knowledge, and attitudes—that students will need. Although this goal may not be totally attainable, in a subsequent chapter we will present an approach to teaching—the mastery approach—that attempts to adjust the instructional procedures used with students so that each student can attain the skills, knowledge and attitudes we want them to achieve. In this chapter, we will describe ways of analyzing the abilities of our students and indicating how objectives might be modified in order to be more consistent with their abilities.

MAJOR CONCEPTS AND EXAMPLES

Just as it is important to specify your objectives, because they are statements that tell you where your students are going, it is equally important for you to know where your students are starting. Usually this starting point is referred to as their prerequisite skills, that is, those skills that students must have in order to begin your instruction.

You are probably most familiar with the term prerequisite in connection with college courses which have prerequisites. Often the prerequisites are listed as other courses, but seldom are they listed in terms of specific knowledge or experience you must have before beginning a course. Nearly all of us have had the experience of taking the wrong section of a prerequisite course, a section that did not really prepare us for the higher level courses that followed. Such situations point to the fact that in planning effective instruction, it is extremely important to identify exactly what prerequisite skills, knowledge, and attitudes students must possess before they begin your instruction.

In order to identify the prerequisites your students should possess before you begin teaching them a particular skill, knowledge, or attitude, simply ask yourself, "What do the students have to know, or be able to do before I start teaching them?" While this is a fairly straightforward question, it requires some analysis to identify the appropriate skills, knowledge, and attitudes. Too often, we assume that students have the skills they need to begin learning a particular topic.

The concept of prerequisites is perhaps more easily understood in the context of teaching something like long division. If we assume that the students are ready for instruction on this topic, then they certainly must have the following as a minimum set of prerequisites: the ability to add, subtract, and multiply. If they do not have these skills, then they will have a great deal of difficulty using the procedures that we teach them for doing long division because such procedures will include the use of these skills.

If we can assume that our students already possess the prerequisites we identify, then there is no need to modify our objectives or the instruction that will follow. If, however, we determine that our students do not have the prerequisites, then we must modify our objectives by adding additional skills to our list of those to be taught in order to compensate for the prerequisites the students do not have. If we fail to do so, our instruction will invariably fail. In the problem scenario, Ms. Helmer has an objective that requires many prerequisite skills that the low ability students apparently do not have.

When we talk about prerequisites, we are talking about very specific skills that students need to have before they begin our instruction. For now, let us return to our classification of students in terms of above average, average, and below average. How does that affect our consideration of prerequisites? Clearly, those students who are considered gifted have a larger pool of knowledge and skills than those in the lower categories. We can, with greater certainty, presume that they have the prerequisites that will be necessary for the instruction we are to provide. Similarly, if we are dealing with below-average students, we may conclude that they are less likely to have retained the prerequisite skills and knowledge required for beginning instruction on a new skill. In such a situation, while we may not have to modify our objective, it will be critically important to help our students recall the prerequisites as they begin to learn the new information.

Another way in which we must modify our instruction for below-average learners is to accommodate their particular learning strategies. Usually such learners have some difficulty understanding written information and are not good at remembering that information. Therefore, we may need to modify our objectives by breaking them into smaller steps, which can be achieved and retained more easily. In our example, before Ms. Helmer taught her students how to solve percentage problems, perhaps she should have reviewed fractions with them and provided them with some real world applications of percentages. In addition, perhaps the instruction should have been less formal and more interactive in order to stimulate student participation.

Identifying Students' Prerequisite Skills

The assessment of skills, knowledge, and attitudes does not continue on a formal basis throughout the academic year because so much of our instruction builds on the preceding instruction. Thus, when we test students following one segment of instruction, the results of the test provide us with information regarding how well students are prepared for the next segment. So, in one sense, when we give a test at the end of one instructional unit, it not only serves as an indication of what the student learned in that unit, but also as an indication of whether the student has the necessary prerequisites to proceed to the next unit. The key issue then becomes whether we provide additional instructional time to those students who have not acquired the necessary prerequisites. Mastery learning is the name given to an instructional approach designed to provide learners with the instructional time they need. This approach is discussed in greater detail in Chapter Nine.

Perhaps the most common method for assessing prerequisite skills and knowledge involves administering a pretest to students. This test may have been given at the end of the last school year, but it is more effective if it is given just prior to the beginning of instruction on a particular topic. The content of the test is not what you are going to teach, but rather it contains items to assess the knowledge and skills students should have when you begin instruction.

If some of the prerequisites your students must possess are motor skills or attitudes, then rather than giving them a written test, it is more appropriate to observe the students as they demonstrate some of these prerequisite skills.

In the next chapter, we will describe how you can go about designing tests to assess prerequisite skills. For the moment, it is important to recognize that knowing where your students are starting from is an important aspect of the instructional planning process, and that the results of this analysis may lead to an immediate modification of the goals and objectives in your instructional plan.

Modifying the Instructional Plan

It is important to analyze your students' skills, knowledge, and attitudes right from the beginning as you develop your instructional plans. If you find that you have a homogeneous group of average or above-average students with the same basic knowledge and attitudes, then it may be safe for you to proceed to build an instructional plan around your objectives. However, if your analysis suggests that your students may lack the necessary prerequisites, then you have the obligation to add those skills, in the form of objectives, to the list of skills that must be taught to your students. If your analysis indicates that students may not have the proper attitudes for receiving your instruction, then it may not be necessary to modify your objectives, but rather to take this into consideration as you develop your instructional activities.

In this chapter we have been particularly concerned with examining the relationship between objectives (which represent the outcomes of instruction) and prerequisites (which represent where students are starting from), and the impact this analysis has on changes that need to be made to your objectives. In subsequent chapters we will find that this analysis of student skills, knowledge, and attitudes also will be important as you develop tests for different types of students, and particularly as you design instructional activities. As you will see, tests and instructional activities are greatly influenced by the general ability and specific knowledge of your students.

PRACTICE

1. Which of the following appear to be appropriate prerequisites for the instructional activities listed?
   A. Draw a straight line before learning to letter.
   B. Add before learning to multiply.
   C. Interpret decimals before learning to compute percents.
   D. Write paragraphs before learning to identify musical instruments.
2. How would you go about determining if students had acquired certain prerequisite skills, knowledge, or attitudes?
3. How would you modify your instructional objectives if you found that
   A. your students were quite low in ability?
   B. your students were above average in ability?
   C. your students knew about half the prerequisites for your instruction?
   D. your students fell into two general groups: half of the students knew the prerequisites for your instruction, the other half did not?
   E. your students had poor attitudes about the content that you were about to teach?
4. It is generally not necessary for teachers to continually assess students prerequisite skills, knowledge, and attitudes for every lesson throughout the year. Why?

FEEDBACK

1. For each of the first three situations, namely teaching lettering, multiplication, and percents, the skills which have been indicated are some of the prerequisites that students must possess in order for them to acquire the new skills that will be taught to them. However, in our last example it is not necessary to know that students can write paragraphs before teaching them to identify musical instruments. It may be desirable if they know how to write paragraphs, but it is not a logical prerequisite skill to learning to identify musical instruments. It is necessary to be on guard for false prerequisites—skills that sometimes are nice to know, but certainly are not required to learn the skills that we are about to teach.

2. The most common way of identifying whether students possess certain prerequisite skills or knowledge is to provide the students with a written test covering those prerequisites. This should be done prior to the time that students receive instruction on the new task. As for the other types of prerequisites, it is a good idea to ask students to perform the prerequisite motor skills or put the students in situations where they must exhibit certain prerequisite attitudes.

3. A. With a lower ability group, you may find that you have to add additional objectives as prerequisites if the group does not already possess them, and you may also find that you need to break larger objectives down into smaller steps for these particular learners.
   B. With above average students, it is unlikely that you will make any changes in your objectives, unless you determine that your students already possess the skills that you intend to teach them. You would then add additional objectives on more advanced topics.
   C. If you found that your students had only half the prerequisites they needed, then the logical thing to do would be to add the prerequisites they do not

have to your list of objectives for the lesson. That is, first teach the students those prerequisite skills which they must have in order for them to learn the skills to be taught in your lesson.

D. The situation in which half the students have the prerequisite skills and the other half do not poses a difficult but common situation for the teacher. One solution is to place the students into two groups, based on their prior knowledge, and provide different instruction to the two groups. Or, we can teach all of the students the prerequisite skills, knowing that half of them do not need that instruction. There are several ways in which your instructional activities can be modified to accommodate the situation, but the typical solution is to add the prerequisites as objectives for your instruction.

E. If your students had negative attitudes about the content you were about to teach, rather than changing your objectives you might decide to overcome the problem by building some highly motivating activities into your instruction. This approach to overcoming negative attitudes will be discussed in greater detail in Chapter Seven.

4. By the middle of the school year, you will be fairly certain about the general ability of the students in your classes, along with their knowledge of the specific prerequisites for the topics for which you will be providing instruction. However, during the early part of the school year, or before you begin instruction on an entirely new topic, it is very important that you test students on the prerequisite skills, knowledge, and attitudes required for the new topic.

APPLICATION

Describe in detail the characteristics of the students who will receive the instruction you are planning. Categorize the students as above average, average, or below average. Indicate the prerequisites for each of your objectives and state how you will determine if the students have them. Indicate how your objectives might have to be modified in light of your analysis of your students.

SUMMARY

In this chapter we have described how important it is to be aware of student prerequisite skills, knowledge, and attitudes as you plan effective instruction. We have defined prerequisites as those skills which students must have in order to begin receiving your instruction. It may be necessary to develop test instruments or observation plans to determine if students do, in fact, have the specific prerequisites that are required for your instruction. We have also described the importance of being aware of differences in the general learning abilities of above-average, average, and below-average learners, and we have discussed the types of modifications to objectives that might be made in light of the characteristics of these three groups of learners. The way in which tests are written and administered, and the type of instructional activities that will be incorporated in the classroom are also likely to be affected by the types of learners with whom you are working.

CHAPTER FIVE
DEVELOPING TESTS

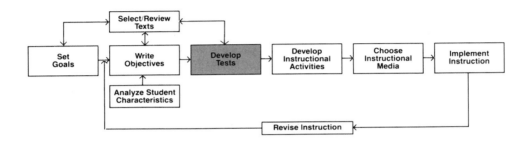

Tests cannot be viewed separately from the instructional process. They are our means of assessing whether students have achieved our goals and objectives, and therefore, our tests must be consistent with our goals and objectives.

PROBLEM SCENARIO

Mr. Jefferson just completed a unit on the Russian Revolution and wants to test his students to find out how much they have learned. There is a test provided in the teacher's guide for the social studies textbook he is using. However, as he reviews the test, Mr. Jefferson notes that all of the test items are multiple choice and, for some reason, that bothers him. He can't decide whether to use the test or to write another one. How can he decide if the test items in the teachers' guide he has are appropriate, and if they are not, what kind of items should be written?

CHAPTER OBJECTIVES

The objectives for this chapter are that you will be able to

1. describe the various purposes for using tests
2. determine if test items match objectives
3. write assessments to match given objectives

BACKGROUND INFORMATION

The terms *testing* and *evaluation* are loaded with emotional connotation. We have encountered few people who really enjoy being tested or being evaluated. None of us, it seems, likes to be on the receiving end of tests. However, there is every indication that tests will continue to play an important role in education.

As more and more states become involved in identifying the competencies, or skills, that students in various grade levels must possess, the emphasis on a relatively new approach to testing has increased. This approach involves developing tests that are designed to determine whether students have acquired the various skills that have been identified in the competency statements. Although this manner of developing tests may seem quite reasonable, it is not the traditional way in which tests have been developed. The traditional approach involved creating very difficult items that could be used to rank students in terms of their knowledge of the content area. The items were never intended to be representative of all the knowledge and skills in the area.

Because the new approach to testing focuses on whether students have acquired specific skills, it is very important that the test items that are developed for such tests do assess a student's ability to perform the specified skills. In other words, a test item must measure a student's ability to perform the same behavior as specified in a particular objective. This is often called objective-referenced or criterion-referenced testing. In this chapter, we will describe how to develop test items and other assessment (testing) tools that *match* objectives by requiring students to demonstrate the behaviors described in given objectives.

MAJOR CONCEPTS AND EXAMPLES

There are a number of reasons for testing students:

1. assigning grades to students
2. determining what students know in order to provide appropriate remediation
3. identifying ineffective portions of instruction

Perhaps the most common reason for testing is to assign grades. It is often assumed that the grading of students serves to motivate them to perform at their best. We are all aware of situations in which we have put in an extra effort in order to earn a particularly important grade. We cannot overlook the importance of grades as a motivating factor for many, but certainly not all, students.

Today, however, there are other important reasons for testing students. One is to determine student progress toward the achievement of particular skills. After taking a test designed for such purposes, students can be given specific feedback that is designed to help them master the skills they failed to attain. For example, on a test involving the addition of fractions with common denominators, it is noted that a student is adding the denominators as well as the numerators, incorrectly thinking that $\frac{1}{4} + \frac{1}{4} = \frac{2}{8}$. More important than a grade on this test, is the specific feedback the student should receive. In the example with fractions, the nature of the student's error should be noted and he should be provided with a review of the proper way of adding two fractions with the same denominator. In this case, test items are not being used as a means of making a judgment about the student, but rather as a means of helping the student identify a weakness in his understanding of the content, and as a means of pointing the student in a direction that will be helpful in remediating that weakness.

In a similar fashion, test data can be used to help the teacher. Usually it can be assumed that when most of the students in a class do poorly on items for a particular objective, there has been something about the instruction that has gone wrong. Often the data from well-designed test items can help us pinpoint what those problems are and may suggest revisions that will make the instruction more effective in the future.

Testing can be used not only to motivate students and to assign them a grade, but can also be used very effectively to determine student progress in achieving certain skills and to provide appropriate remediation. Furthermore, tests can be used to provide data to teachers to improve their instruction.

Who Develops Test Items?

Professionals who work for companies that produce tests or for state-level testing programs, spend much of their time writing and revising test items. They have to create large pools of test items and to examine the data from thousands of students who have taken the tests. In addition to the items prepared by these professional test-makers, many test items are written by textbook writers who provide test items for the chapters in their books. These test items usually appear in the teachers' guide for the text. It is important to note, however, that textbook writers are not necessarily expert test writers, and the items that they produce may or may not be good assessments of the behaviors they are trying to teach. Furthermore, in many textbook series, the test items that appear in the accompanying teachers' guides may not be written by the textbook authors, but by others who may not be totally familiar with the content of the text.

Another source of test items is the classroom teacher. Teacher education programs have traditionally included little, if any, formal training in the development of test items. Most teachers, because of this lack of training, have inadequate understanding of the concepts underlying sound test development and, consequently, end up developing tests like those that their teachers gave them. We hope that the new approach to developing test items, as described in this chapter, will begin to remedy this situation.

How Do You Recognize a Good Test Item?

This is a difficult question; not one that has an easy answer. Our basic position is that a good test item is one that measures what it is intended to measure. This is basically the concept of the *validity* of a test or a test item. Putting this notion into terms we have been working with, if there is a match between the behavior described in an objective and the behavior assessed by a test item designed to measure student attainment of that objective, then it may be said that the test item is valid. For example, if an objective indicates that "the student will be able to add two two-digit numbers," then a valid test item would be one that requires the student to add two two-digit numbers. It would be inappropriate to ask students to add two three-digit numbers. Is the validity of the item affected by whether the two numbers are listed vertically or horizontally? Not unless the objective specifies the way in which the numbers should be arranged.

In a system of the sort presented in this book, you begin with goals and objectives, and your objectives then serve as the basis upon which to develop test items. The verb in an objective describes the kind of behavior that you expect from your learners and that you would assess on a test. For example, if the objective states that the student will be able to "list," then we would expect that the test item in turn would ask the student to "list" some information. While it is not always possible to use the verb in the objective directly in the construction of the test items, it does give us the key as to which kind of item will be appropriate to measure the objective.

Let's review the four domains of objectives and the kinds of test items that are most often used to assess the objectives in those domains.

Assessment of Knowledge

Knowledge objectives require students to recognize or recall information that they have already encountered. Here we are asking the student to either state, describe, or list some information; or to select from an array of possible answers, such as would be the case with a multiple choice question. Therefore, knowledge items might require the student to list the two primary political parties in the United States or to select, from a list, the food with the highest amount of carbohydrates. In the first case we are requiring the student to generate the answer by completing a question, and in the second case we are asking the student to simply recognize the information. In both cases, we are assuming that the specific information has been taught and it is a matter of recalling or recognizing it.

Assessment of Intellectual Skills

Here again, we find ourselves predominately using either multiple choice or completion test items. Typically, when the objective has to do with learning about concepts, we can use multiple choice items in which the student is required to select examples of that concept. For example, if we were to have an objective stating that children will be able to recognize those animals that are members of the cat family, we could provide a question in which the names or pictures of various animals are presented and we could ask the student to select, or identify, those in the cat family.

As we move to the next level of intellectual skills, namely rule-using, we are more likely to have the students complete an answer rather than to pick a multiple choice answer, although that is not always the case. For example, suppose we want our students to use rules to determine how to set a boat's sail in order to reach a certain point when they are given the current position of the boat and the direction of the wind. Our first choice would be to ask each student to actually sail a boat under various conditions. This would combine a motor skill with an intellectual skill. If this is not possible, then we would have to consider less direct indications of their skills. We would either assess our students' ability to perform this task by listing a number of sail positions and asking the students to select the correct one or to describe the correct sail position. In either case, we would be asking the students to use a rule in order to determine how to set the sail.

If we progress to the next level of intellectual skills, namely problem solving, then we are even more likely to have students respond to a completion item. For example, we may want our students to be able to describe how to navigate a sailboat around a land mass in order to reach a point on the other side. In all likelihood, we would write an item in which they would be given a description of a situation with a sailboat, and they would be asked to describe how they would sail it.

Assessment of Motor Skills

In many situations, a relatively informal approach is taken to assessing motor skills. The instructor simply observes students performing the skill and decides whether they have or have not been successful. Whether or not the instructor is aware of it, he or she is, in fact, using a mental checklist to determine if the student has been successful. A more objective approach would be to have a written checklist, or set of criteria, available for judging the adequacy of each student's performance. The checklist might simply be a list of the characteristics of what you would consider to be a successful performance. For example, a checklist for assessing the adequacy of a tennis serve might include such items as "Was the ball tossed upwards properly?" "Did the learner fully extend his or her arm during the swing?" "Did the ball clear the net?", and "Did the ball land in the appropriate section of the court?"

With any motor skill, the objective should indicate whether we are evaluating the process itself (that is, the execution of the skill), the result of the performance of the skill, or both (as was the case in our tennis serving example). For example, if we are teaching diving, it is almost certain that the performance of the various components of the dive will be evaluated in order to determine whether the student has been successful or not. On the other hand, if we are judging a student's ability to make a ceramic pot, we might not be as concerned with the specific steps that are followed in the process of making the pot, but rather would make our assessment on the basis of the quality of the final product, the pot. These are decisions which you, the teacher, must make as you develop your objectives and the assessments for them.

Assessment of Attitudes

As we have indicated earlier, we consider attitudes to be feelings and beliefs that are reflected in tendencies to act in particular ways in given situations. First of all, it is critical that students actually have the behaviors that we wish them to demonstrate. Then we can determine if they choose, in fact, to execute those behaviors. Therefore, when assessing an attitude it is important to provide the student with a situation in which that attitude or the behavior which reflects that attitude would be appropriately displayed. Usually, this can best be assessed through direct observation.

We may also wish to assess our students' knowledge of the situation which is related to their attitudes. For example, if we attempted to teach attitudes about religious freedom and religious tolerance, we might want to provide some test items dealing with our students' knowledge of the various religious faiths that they might encounter in their city. This would indicate if they are even aware of the religious beliefs of which we would like them to be tolerant. If we wanted to teach young children to share, we would want to determine if they could describe what it means "to share."

Our purpose for reviewing the various domains of learning outcomes with regard to testing is to point out that the first step in developing the test items for any objective is to identify what domain the objective is in. Once you have done so, you can narrow down the type of item that would best assess the behavior described in the objective. We have summarized this information below.

TYPICAL TESTING PROCEDURES

Domain	Types of Testing and Assessment
Knowledge	Multiple choice, completion
Intellectual Skills	Multiple choice, completion, essay, product
Motor Skills	Checklist, success of executing skill
Attitudes	Observation of behavior, questionnaire about behavior, various assessments of knowledge associated with the attitudes

We can use this summary to help us consider the problem posed in the opening scenario in which Mr. Jefferson is bothered that the items provided in his teachers' guide are all multiple choice. We know that he should examine the relationship between his specific objectives and the items and determine if there is a match. There may well be a match, and items should not be criticized simply because they are in a multiple-choice format. If, however, Mr. Jefferson finds that the objectives and items don't match, then he will have to write new ones. The techniques for doing so are discussed in the next section.

Writing Test Items

We know that in many situations tests are written after the instruction is presented in order to have a test that best reflects what was actually taught. In such situations, we are letting the instruction, rather than the objectives, dictate what appears on a test. Our suggestion is that we need to rearrange this situation. Our model indicates that the goals and objectives for the instruction must indicate the nature of the test items that will be used to determine if the goals and objectives have been achieved. Then we present instruction that is consistent with the goals, objectives, and test items.

We also might make a comment about the terms *test* and *test items*. While we have used these terms extensively in our discussion, perhaps better terms would have been *assessments* and *assessing student-learning outcomes*. A test item implies a paper-and-pencil type of performance on the part of the student, when in fact many of our objectives call for other kinds of behavior, such as the demonstration of a motor skill or an attitude. The best way to assess these behaviors is not by giving students a paper-and-pencil test, but rather by observing students perform a motor skill, exhibit an attitude or produce a product like a report. We will continue to use the terms *test* and *test items*, but you should be aware that we are really using those terms in a broader context of assessing the behaviors that are described in objectives and developing an assessment situation that is most appropriate for that behavior.

In this brief text we cannot provide a complete set of rules on how to develop various types of tests and test items. We encourage you to check other sources to get a more thorough understanding of this process. Nonetheless, it is our contention that the most crucial step in test-item construction is being aware of the behavior described in an objective and writing test items that assess a student's ability to perform that behavior. In writing such items, however, it is important to know some of the basic rules of good test-item construction. Therefore, in the paragraphs that follow we will provide you with some basic information that should help you to develop very appropriate test items for classroom testing purposes.

If the behavior in your objective indicates that the student will "identify" or "select" something, then often a multiple-choice item or series of multiple-choice items can be used to assess the student. When developing multiple-choice items there are two very basic rules to follow. The first rule is to put as much information as possible in the stem, that is, that portion of the question that the students read before they select their answer. In other words, don't put just a few words in the stem and then load up all of the alternatives with many words. In fact, do just the reverse. Try to minimize the length of the alternatives.

Good item:

In the United States, airplane speed is most enhanced by the wind when planes are flying in which direction?

1. north
2. south
3. east
4. west

Poor item:
Planes fly

1. slower when they head north
2. faster when they head west
3. faster when they fly east
4. about the same speed regardless of direction

The second rule in developing multiple-choice items is to have all of the alternative answers be of approximately the same length, and none of them should contain particular cues which will result in someone choosing the correct answer who did not really know it.

Good item:

In the story *Mrs. Smith Went to Arizona*, her primary concern seemed to be

1.   her financial security
2.   her sons and daughters
3.   her job prospects
4.   her home and neighborhood

Poor item:

If John rode his bike for 2½ hours at a steady rate of 15 miles per hour, to the nearest ½ mile, how far would he go?

1.   30 minutes
2.   35 blocks
3.   37.5 miles
4.   40 hours

If the behavior in your objective indicates that the student will "name" or "state" something, then a completion item is appropriate. When developing completion items, it has been our experience that you can get a much better indication of what students really know by asking them to respond to specific questions, rather than completing a statement by filling in a blank space. For example, rather than asking students to complete the statement "The Battle of the Bulge was fought in ————," it would be better to ask the students: "In what year was the Battle of the Bulge fought?" The completion question could be answered with either a date or a location.

If your objective calls for the student to "discuss," "describe," or "explain" something, then an essay question is the type of test item you should employ. Frequently, the item can be worded using much the same language as the objective. For example, if the objective states that "The student will describe the ecological principles that should be employed to maintain a marsh area," then your essay question might simply state "In two or three paragraphs, describe the ecological principles that should be employed to maintain a marsh area." An essay question does not necessarily require a long, complicated answer.

In addition to developing the essay question itself, you should also develop a list of criteria you will use to determine whether or not the student has correctly answered the question. For example, before your students respond to the essay question about marshes, you should have a clear idea of the features of the answer you want them to list. Perhaps one such feature would be that the student clearly described three of the eco- logical principles discussed in class.

If your objective requires the student to perform a motor skill, then the use of a performance checklist is in order. When developing such checklists, you should be certain to list each of the major steps necessary to perform the motor skill. It is not easy to determine exactly what is meant by a major step, and we can obviously err in the direction of having too few or too many steps in our checklist. Nonetheless, when you develop a checklist to assess the performance of a motor skill, the important thing is to try to identify those critical components that are likely to result in either success or failure in the overall performance of the skill.

With attitude objectives, if we can't actually observe the student mak- ing an attitudinal choice, we will use a questionnaire. Such questionnaires consist of items that do not necessarily have a right or wrong answer, but rather measure how students feel about various topics. Much has been written about questionnaire construction. The most important aspect is to avoid writing questions that will lead students to respond as they think you want them to (by giving you the socially acceptable answer), rather than in accordance with how they really feel. In other words, the questionnaire should be as value-free as possible and should provide the respondents with the opportunity to honestly describe what they do or how they feel. If a student, or anyone else, is filling out a questionnaire in which there is a clear indication of what the socially acceptable or desired answer is, the tendency is to give that answer or to give no answer at all.

A good item to ask on a questionnaire related to a human relations objective:

> Give an example of a situation that occurred this week in which you helped another student with a problem.

Poor items to ask on a questionnaire related to a human relations objective:

> Were you cheerful when working with other students this week?
>
> Do you believe that everyone should be treated the same?

One of the important factors in determining the success of a test is trying out that test in advance with one of your learners or someone who is similar to those learners. It has been our experience that there are often as many or more problems with the tests given in an instructional setting as there are with the instruction itself. Since we are going to make important decisions about our learners and the quality of our instruction on the basis of our test data, it is critically important that the test items say what we want them to say. The best way of determining whether this is so is to try out test items with learners.

When you are constructing a test and you know what the right answer is, it is easy to believe that a test item says exactly what you think it says. However, when your words are translated onto paper and are typed and appear before the student, it is absolutely amazing how many alternative interpretations can be given to something that you think is very straightforward. Therefore, it is exceedingly important that any test that you develop be tried out with someone, preferably a student like those in your class. Perhaps you can use a student who was in your class the previous year. In addition, trying your test with another teacher, or a secretary, will often prove to be helpful. In short, have someone else help find the inevitable problems that appear in any instrument of this sort. Use that person's reactions to revise and improve your test in order to make sure it really is testing that which you think it is testing.

How Is a Test Developed?

In our discussion thus far, we have been primarily focusing on individual test items and the importance of those items reflecting the behavior described in an objective. However, at some point items must be put together in the form of a test. In this regard, there are two extremely important decisions that must be made by you, the test developer. The first includes the length and specificity of the directions that accompany the test and the second involves determining how many items are to be included.

We are all frustrated at times by vague instructions at the beginning of a test. We are already a little anxious about having to take the test and perhaps somewhat insecure about our knowledge about what is being tested. Now we read the directions and find out that we really don't know what we are being asked to do.

We can't overemphasize the importance of being extremely explicit, clear, and simple with the directions for any test that you are going to develop. For example, you should let students know such things as whether they should attempt to answer every question, how much time they will have to complete the test, and the point value of each test item or cluster of test items. This is the kind of information you would want if you were taking a test, and your students certainly should have it as well.

An equally important question is how many test items are needed to determine if your students have really mastered your objectives. While there is no hard and fast answer to this question, there are some rules-of-thumb that have evolved over time by people who have developed classroom tests, and these rules are related to the four domains of learning. In the knowledge domain, if our objective is to identify the capital of the state of Texas, then there is basically only one question we can ask a student about this objective, namely, "What is the capital of the state of Texas?" We might use a completion item or we might use multiple choice, depending on how the objective is stated, but we certainly would not ask that question more than once. In general, then, if your objective involves the recall or recognition of knowledge, then you need ask only one question for each fact you hope your students have memorized. If the number of facts is quite large, then you will have to test only a sample of those facts.

If your objective involves an intellectual skill, then it is likely that more than one item will be needed to determine if your students have mastered the objective. To be more specific, it has often been suggested that at least three items be used to assess student attainment of an intellectual skill. If we refer to our objective of adding two two-digit numbers, we might use three items like these:

1.   43   2.   37   3.   51
      +52   +55   +89

If a student can respond correctly to two of these three items, then the student probably is not guessing, but has actually mastered the intellectual skill. While the role of chance may be operating, particularly in multiple choice situations, there is sufficient evidence to suggest that three items is sufficient for typical classroom testing of intellectual skills.

Now let's consider a motor skill. While you have developed a checklist that describes the steps in executing that procedure and/or describes the quality of the product that will result from that motor skill, you still must determine how many times the student will be asked to perform the behavior. You may have decided this when you wrote the criterion portion of your objective, but regardless of whether you did so or not, the key question you must ask yourself is "How many times (or what percentage of the time) must a student perform this behavior correctly before I am satisfied that the student really mastered the skill?" Unfortunately, there are no rules for answering this question, so you must rely on your own judgment and experience.

As indicated earlier, an attitude is usually assessed either through observation or through the use of an attitude questionnaire. If we observe the student, we must decide how many times he or she must choose a particular behavior before we are willing to say that the student has acquired the desired attitude. If we use an attitude questionnaire, our decision is even harder. We must decide how we will tabulate the student's responses and how we will interpret the results of that tabulation. Again, there are no specific rules to follow in this situation. As you can see, accurate assessment of student attitudes is a particularly difficult issue.

PRACTICE

1. Describe at least three major purposes for testing students after they have completed instruction.

2. Listed below are a number of objectives (with the criteria omitted) and test items. In each case, indicate if the test item adequately measures the objective. If not, write a better test item.
    A. Objective: Define justice.

    Test item: Define justice.

    B. Objective: Describe the two-party system.

    Test item: Select the party of the current president of the United States:
    a. Democrat
    b. Republican
    c. Labor
    d. Independent

    C. Objective: From a given list of food items, identify foods that are high in sugar.

    Test item: Circle the foods listed below that are high in sugar:
    a. bananas
    b. potatoes
    c. chocolate
    d. orange juice

    D. Objective: Be able to convert from scientific to standard notation.

    Test item: State the rule for converting from scientific to standard notation.

    E. Given a hypothetical monthly income, the student will be able to realistically allocate funds to basic items in the family budget.

    Test item: In the United States, how much money is required per month to live at a minimum standard of living?

3. Listed below are five objectives. Read each objective carefully and then write a test item that you think would assess that objective.
    A. Given a road map of the state of Florida, locate the major cities.
    B. Be able to execute a successful serve in volleyball.
    C. Be able to state the second law of thermodynamics.
    D. Be able to discuss the impact of high technology on the economy of the state of California.
    E. Be able to develop a plan for implementing instruction for a particular objective.

FEEDBACK

1. One of the major purposes of testing is to rank order students in order to assign them grades or to determine an award-winner, but other purposes related to instruction may be of equal importance. One such purpose is to provide feedback to learners, particularly about skills they have not performed well. This feedback can help students identify the remediation they need in order to improve their performance. Another purpose of testing is to provide feedback to the teacher about ineffective instruction that should be improved before the next time it is presented.

2. The items relating to the definition of justice (objective A) and the identification of food that is high in sugar (objective C) seem to be appropriate.

    Objective B called for students to describe the two-party system. The test item, however, merely asked the students to identify the political party of the president. Obviously, the behavior called for by the test item does not match the behavior specified in the objective. An appropriate test item for this objective would have been an essay question asking students to describe the two-party system.

    Because objective D indicated that the student would actually compute the answer by converting from scientific notation to standard notation, it was inappropriate to ask the student to simply state the rule for doing so. We often mistakenly believe that if a student can state a rule, then the student should be able to apply it. However, research has indicated that this is simply not the case. Sometimes students can state the rule, but not actually apply it; and in other cases, we find that students can apply rules, but become confused when asked to state them. Therefore, in this particular case, the appropriate test item would have been a number expressed in scientific notation and directions asking the student to convert that number to standard notation.

    The test item for objective E asked students to indicate how much money is required to have a minimum standard of living. This does not assess a student's ability to realistically allocate funds to basic items in a family budget, which was the behavior specified in our objective. It would have been much more appropriate to give the student a monthly dollar figure and a list of standard household budgetary items, such as housing, transportation, clothing, and food, and ask the student to distribute the dollars across those categories.

    In those cases in which the test items we provided were inappropriate, you may have written new ones that were somewhat different from the ones we suggested here. The item you wrote may very well be appropriate, provided that it called for the same behavior as specified in the given objective.

3. It is impossible to list *the* correct test item for each of the objectives provided. However, we can suggest the kind of items we think would be appropriate and you can check your answers against ours.

    A. A good item would include a road map of the state of Florida, with all of the cities shown in their proper location. The directions for the item would ask the student to circle the major cities in the state. Perhaps the directions would also indicate the number of major cities that were to be circled. Another possibility, requiring a more difficult behavior on the part of your students, would be to give the students a blank outline map of the state of Florida and ask them to list the name of each major city and place an X next to the location of each one. Clearly there is room for interpretation as to what the word "locate" means in this particular situation.

    B. We would hope that you would develop a checklist that would indicate the major steps in executing an effective serve in volleyball. Your checklist would probably involve such things as holding the ball, throwing the ball in the air, moving the arm in a particular pattern with the eventual result of having the ball arrive in the desired area on the other side of the net. This is an example of a motor skill in which both the process and the result, or outcome, can be judged. You must decide if both the process and the result must be acceptable.

    C. In stating the second law of thermodynamics, it would be quite appropriate to simply ask the student to "state the second law of thermodynamics," and leave a blank space for the answer.

D. The objective indicates that students will be able to discuss the impact of high technology on California's economy. We assume that this is a knowledge objective that is simply asking students to recall information that they have learned from the text or from classroom discussions. Therefore the test item can be written in a fashion almost identical to that of the objective, namely, "Discuss at least four important ways in which the introduction of high technology has affected the economy of the state of California." Then leave space for the student to respond to this question.

E. In asking the student to develop a plan for implementing instruction for a particular objective, you would state the question in a fashion very similar to the objective. However, you would have to decide who chooses the content of the objective, you or the student. In other words, you might state that the student should develop an instructional plan for teaching long division, or you might state that the student should develop an instructional plan for any objective he or she chooses. In any event, you would want to have, for your own purposes, a checklist that would (a) list the components that students should include in their instructional plan and, perhaps, (b) describe the criteria you would use to judge the adequacy of the components. You could then use this checklist to judge each student's plan.

APPLICATION

In your instructional plan, you have developed a number of goals and for each goal you have one or more objectives. Those objectives have been modified to reflect the abilities of the students you will be teaching.

At this point, you should write one or more assessment items for each of your objectives. For some objectives, you may need to develop two or three items, while for other objectives, one item will certainly be enough. Put the items together in one assessment instrument, and provide directions to the student at the top of the instrument.

After you have completed the instrument, have a student who might receive your instruction, or someone else, review your test items. See if the person can explain what he or she thinks is being asked for each of your items. Make appropriate revisions in your test items based on the observations of this person.

SUMMARY

In this chapter we have reviewed the overall importance of testing in the process of designing instruction. We have emphasized the fact that test items are extremely important for providing students with an assessment of their progress in mastering objectives, and that test results provide teachers with information regarding the quality of the instruction they have presented, as well as suggest how instruction might be revised in the future.

When we are using a systematic approach to planning instruction, the single most important characteristic of a test item is that it matches the behavior described in the objective the test item is intended to test. We have provided various rules-of-thumb for developing test items and for combining those items into a test. It is especially important to try out the test prior to actually using it in the classroom.

CHAPTER SIX
SELECTING TEXTBOOKS AND OTHER PRINTED MATERIALS

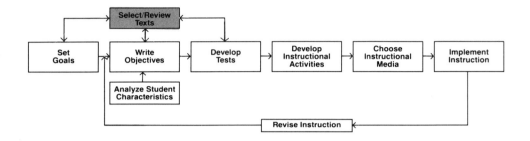

As you go about planning instructional activities for your students, you are likely to be influenced by many factors. We hope these factors will include the characteristics of your students, as well as the goals, objectives, and test items you have identified. However, regardless of the extent to which these factors affect your planning, your textbook is likely to have a major impact upon the instructional decisions you make. Therefore, before we consider the development of instructional activities, we think it is important to focus our attention on textbooks. In this chapter we discuss the role of textbooks in the instructional process and describe a method for evaluating and selecting textbooks.

PROBLEM SCENARIO

The school district has appointed a textbook committee to select a reading series for grades K–6. At their first meeting, committee members are told that nine reading series are available, from which they must select one. Members who are familiar with some of the series express opinions about the quality of the stories and illustrations, and the value of the workbooks that are provided. There is much discussion about how the committee should proceed. How should the committee select the reading series that will be used in the district?

CHAPTER OBJECTIVES

The objectives for this chapter are that you will be able to

1. describe criteria for evaluating textbooks and other printed materials
2. apply the criteria to select a textbook for given objectives and students
3. apply the criteria to select supplementary print materials for given objectives and students

BACKGROUND INFORMATION

It has often been said that "textbooks drive the curriculum." This statement implies that many instructional decisions are based upon the textbook that is used in a particular course or subject area. Indeed, this is often the case; the textbook selected for use in a particular class is likely to have an effect upon decisions about the instructional goals and objectives the class will pursue, the tests the class will be given, and the instructional activities the class will engage in.

The ambiguity of when textbooks are chosen is represented in our diagram of the planning process at the beginning of the chapter; we have placed "Select/Review Text" in a position that indicates that this component may occur at any one of a number of places. Ideally we would like to select the text as part of the development of the instructional activities. However, in reality, this step almost always occurs much earlier in the planning process.

Because textbooks often have a significant influence on instructional plans, it is important that you carefully select the textbooks you will use in your classes. However, if you do not have the opportunity to help select the textbooks that you will use, then it is important to be able to determine the extent to which they are likely to be useful.

Who is involved in the textbook selection process? Until fairly recently, few teachers were given the opportunity to help select the textbooks that would be used in their classrooms. Fortunately, this situation is changing. Now, in many states, more and more teachers are serving on district or county level committees that are involved in textbook selection and adoption.

Another shift in the process involves how textbooks are reviewed. The "thumb test" was the name given to a common method for reviewing textbooks. While somewhat of an exaggeration, this method involves simply flipping through a text to examine the pictures and the layout in order to come to a decision about that text. Fortunately, few districts use the thumb test to select textbook materials. Most states and districts use specific criteria, which are agreed on in advance, for selecting instructional materials.

This attention to textbook selection comes at a time when most teachers have not been provided with any form of training in the process of textbook selection. It has been the case that many other topics have pressed this one to the sidelines in terms of coverage in teacher education programs. The argument has been that very few teachers ever really get a chance to participate in textbook selection, so why should a great deal of time be spent on the skill. Now, however, the situation has changed; today it seems much more important that teachers acquire skills in the area of textbook selection.

Much research published in recent years indicates the critical role that textbooks play in the classroom. Because of their importance, the textbooks that are selected should support the goals and objectives that our students are expected to attain. Similarly, other types of supplementary print materials (such as workbooks) used in the classroom should be appropriate for the goals and objectives that have been identified. Therefore, the criteria used for the selection of texts should also be applied to the selection of supplementary materials.

MAJOR CONCEPTS AND EXAMPLES

Before considering some specific criteria that you might use in selecting a textbook, let's briefly discuss some of the problems with typical textbook selection procedures. One problem is that when textbooks are being selected, there is a great temptation to focus almost exclusively on the content in the book. If what is said is inaccurate or incomplete, then we certainly don't want to use the text. However, an exclusive focus on content is not sufficient in evaluating a text. There are other aspects of a text that are equally important to consider. We will discuss these shortly.

Another problem involves the reputation some publishing companies have established. Many times, a publishing company has established a reputation for quality in a particular content area. It's often very tempting to simply acknowledge the quality of what that publisher has done in the past and, with very little thought, adopt the publisher's new textbook in that area. While some textbook publishers are flattered that this occurs, it is not fair to the others who are also attempting to place quality books on the market. Resist the temptation to simply select the text based on the reputation of the publisher or the personality of the sales representative who has been so kind and helpful to you in the past.

Another problem that is often mentioned by people who have served on textbook selection committees is that there simply is not enough time available to properly conduct the selection process. Committees often do not have enough time to adequately review all the textbooks they should consider. In such instances, we suggest that the committee members go through some quick elimination process that brings the number of texts to review down to four or five. These texts can then be given the detailed analysis they deserve. On the other hand, if committee members feel that a large number of texts should be reviewed in detail, then they should insist that time be made available for them to carry out this critical task. For if, as has been claimed, 95 percent of what goes on in the classroom is influenced in one way or the other by the textbook, then the selection of a textbook is probably the single most important decision that is made with regard to the eventual effectiveness of your instruction.

Categories of Criteria

What criteria should you use to select textbooks? We would like to recommend a set of criteria for textbook selection that has been derived from the criteria used by the state and district textbook selection committees in Florida.

These criteria are presented in Table 6.1. Listed under each criterion are a few questions you might ask in order to determine the quality of a textbook. The criteria are representative of almost all of the criteria that have been applied by various selection committees throughout the country. The list includes and expands upon some items that we feel are critically important to selecting the best text, but which are not always found in the textbook selection process.

We have divided our criteria into four major categories: content, presentation, instructional design, and classroom use. Some of these headings are self-explanatory, while others will require some comment. We will look at these categories in some detail and then describe how you would actually go about examining textbooks to determine to what extent they meet these criteria.

Content

Content refers to the ideas and specific information contained in the text. Here we are concerned with the accuracy of the information and the extent to which the authors distinguish between fact and interpretation. In those areas in which there are controversies, the authors should explain the nature of the controversy and fairly present both sides of it. We know this is easier said than done. All we have to do is look at the furor raised over textbooks dealing with sex education. What one person might consider to

TABLE 6.1. Criteria for Selecting Textbooks and Supplementary Print Materials

I. Content
1. Is the content accurate?
Is information factually stated?
2. Is the content up-to-date? *No*
Is the copyright date within the last five years?
3. Is the content comprehensive?
Is the content congruent with district and/or state curriculum guidelines?
4. Are social issues treated fairly?
✓ Are ethnic groups, males, and females shown in nonstereotyped roles through words and pictures?

II. Presentation
5. Does the text format help make learning easy?
Do the chapters address a single, main theme?
✓ Do print size and type ensure legibility for the grade level of students?
Do the illustrations reinforce the text?
6. Is the content presented at the appropriate grade level for the intended learners?
Do vocabulary and symbols match grade level of learners?
7. Does the writing style help make learning easy?
Is the tone appropriate for the intended learners?
Are directions and explanations clearly stated?

III. Instructional Design
8. Are the instructional components congruent?
Does the content match the objectives and assessments?
9. Do the instructional characteristics facilitate learning?
Are summaries included in each unit or chapter?
Are practice activities included in the text or teacher's edition?
Do practice activities match the content and skills?
Do practice activities match the test items?
Are motivational activities included?

IV. Classroom Use
10. Are the materials effective with students?
Is there data indicating that students learn from the materials?
Is there data indicating that students like the materials?
11. Is use of the instructional materials compatible with the teaching conditions?
Are preferred settings for conducting instructional activities available in user schools?
Are staff development services available from the publisher?
12. Do the supplementary print materials help make learning easier?
Does the teacher's edition match the content of the student text?
Are workbook activities congruent with the content of the text?
Do users state their satisfaction with the materials?

be a balanced approach, another might consider to be extremely biased. Nonetheless, if you are involved in the textbook selection process, you should try to examine whether a book seems to fairly present both sides of a controversial issue.

A second aspect of examining content is determining whether it is up-to-date, that it presents events that have occurred in the last five years, that it depicts or describes current technology, and that it reflects the current culture through recent photographs and illustrations. It should be noted that we can not rely solely on the copyright date that appears in the front of the text as an indication of the content being up-to-date. It is possible to make very minor changes in a book and come forward with a new copyright date when, in fact, very little of the book has been changed and the content is now out-of-date.

Another characteristic of the content is that it must be comprehensive; it must not ignore important parts of the field that should be covered. The text should certainly cover most, if not all, of the topics that are listed in a curriculum guide or outline provided by the state or district for a particular subject area and grade level. If there are large omissions, then those gaps will have to be filled in some other way.

An important source of information about the content in textbooks is the subject matter specialists. These people, usually university faculty members, often are very aware of the texts that are being published and are aware of the kinds of content orientations that are reflected in the texts. A variety of these specialists, if asked to do so, may be willing to provide you with their reactions to several textbooks. Too often, this very important source of information is overlooked by textbook selection committees.

A critical issue that must be examined is the "social fairness" of textbooks. This area has taken on increasing importance in recent years. There is now a requirement that publishers represent individuals in various age, ethnic, and racial groups, as well as members of the two sexes, as being equal in society, without presenting any stereotypes in terms of their interests, abilities, occupations, physical appearance, or language. Publishers are quite aware of the social fairness issue and you will generally find that they meet this criterion. However, it is an important one to check.

Presentation

Presentation, the second major category of criteria, refers to the actual appearance of the content on the page. We are referring to both the physical appearance and the writing style of the authors.

Examination of the way in which content is presented involves a more detailed analysis than the thumb test. Certainly, we want to check the format of the text to determine that it makes learning easier. To do this, we can look at such things as illustrations to determine if they are directly related to, or reinforcing, what is said in the text. We should also check to make sure that the illustrations are labeled correctly and are clear and understandable to the learner. It is also important to check to see that headings, underlining, and bold print are used to help students identify themes and main ideas within the text.

There is also the broader issue of the appropriateness of the text for the intended learners. Does the style and level of the text meet the needs of the learners who will be using it? One of the ways in which these questions are often answered is in terms of the readability level of the text, expressed as a grade level. Many researchers have argued against the wholesale dependency upon this indicator because the sentence structure of a text can be manipulated to reflect a particular grade level, but in doing so, the effectiveness of the text may be sacrificed.

Here we should note the particular problems faced by the teacher who is trying to select a text for students who are what we have described as below-average learners. Usually such learners are below average with regard to their reading ability, knowledge base, and learning skills. Very few publishers have developed texts specifically for them. Therefore, the teacher is faced with one of three alternatives. The first is to select a text that has been written for students at a lower grade level. This may be effective in some situations, but in others it may be insulting to the learners. Furthermore, in some content areas there simply may not be a text written for a lower grade level. As second or third alternatives, the teacher may either use special supplementary materials or not use text materials at all. Certainly this latter alternative is not an attractive one in terms of trying to help students improve their study skills.

The readability level of the text can tell you whether it is close to the level of your students. Nonetheless, it is important to examine portions of the text to determine if, for example, the paragraphs in the text begin with topic sentences and that the paragraphs include detailed explanations of those topics. Also, the directions and explanations in the text should be clearly stated and the tone of the text should be appropriate for your learners.

Instructional Design

We refer to our third category of criteria as instructional design criteria. These criteria focus on current knowledge regarding the learning process and how this knowledge is incorporated into the text to help the student learn the information presented. Most important among the instructional design criteria is the alignment, or congruence, among the objectives of the text, the content presented, and the tests provided. This type of check is referred to as a skill-alignment check, or a skills trace. The importance of an alignment check is to determine if the text is consistent in its representation of (a) what students should be able to do after studying the text, (b) the assessment of those skills, and (c) the information that is provided with regard to those skills.

If we examine a textbook and find that it has objectives and test items, then we can examine the test items for several of the objectives. If there are no test items that match the objectives, then we should be concerned about the validity of all the items. Similarly, if we examine the content of the text and find little that relates directly to the skills described in the objectives, then we would have to question the overall quality of the textbook. On the other hand, if we find that there is a consistency among the objectives, assessments, and the content, then we can be assured that student learning from the text will be enhanced.

There are other important aspects of instructional design that can be examined. For example, to what extent does the textbook motivate learners to study? Does it present interesting examples? In other words, would the students enjoy using this text? We also know that the use of examples in any learning situation often is critical to the understanding of concepts and rules. Therefore, does a text provide clear, straightforward, and appropriate examples? What about the use of practice? Are appropriate items provided and is there feedback available, either in the text itself or in the teachers' guide? All of these questions relate to instructional design considerations that are important to the overall quality of the textbook.

Classroom Use

While this is a broad category, it refers, in general, to information about the use of these materials in classrooms. This information may be available in a variety of forms. The most important information is data concerning the performance and attitudes of groups of students who previously used the materials. How have students performed on tests that have been developed to specifically assess attainment of the objectives? How do they like the materials? A publisher may have conducted a field trial in which they have collected data of this sort. In addition, the publisher may be able to refer you to teachers in other school districts who have used the textbook and who would be glad to share their perceptions of it. It is also quite common to find that publishers have solicited testimonials from teachers about the text. These are highly appropriate, interesting, and often insightful, and will typically provide quite accurate reflections of how the teachers feel about the book. However, it is unlikely that the publishers will pass along testimonials that reflect negatively on the text!

There are other aspects of classroom use that must be examined. For example, are there any special facilities required to implement this text? Are there laboratory exercises that accompany it? Does the text require the use of special technology, such as computers? While computers may be readily available, it is important to be aware of this requirement prior to the selection of the text, rather than being surprised by it later on.

Another important aspect of the classroom-use category is to examine the supplementary print materials that often accompany a text. Here we are referring specifically to the teachers' edition of the text, and any work-books or other supplementary print materials for the students. Since the latter are often written by authors other than those who wrote the text, there may be a mismatch between the supplementary materials and the main text. Therefore, it is important to check out these supplementary materials with the same diligence that you might use for a skills trace between objectives, test items, and content, to determine if, in fact, the supplementary materials relate directly to the skills taught in the text.

Supplementary Print Materials

In addition to helping you select textbooks, the criteria described in this chapter can help you select supplementary print materials to match the specific skills of the learners who will be in your classes. For example, if you are teaching above-average students you might wish to supplement the content in the regular text with that contained in a more advanced text. Or, with below-average learners you may wish to supplement the content in the text with additional practice activities that might engage their interest more than the activities that appear in the regular text. In any case, when you are considering the use of supplementary print materials, you should judge them in light of the criteria we have already discussed.

When it comes to selecting supplementary print materials, of all the criteria we have discussed, perhaps the single most important one is whether the supplementary materials are consistent with your objectives and with the content presented in the textbook. It is also particularly important to determine if these materials have been effective with similar types of learners in other situations. Perhaps the publishers or other teach-ers will be able to provide you with this kind of information.

Applying the Criteria

Before we go on to describe how you might actually apply these criteria, let us describe how, in general terms, the textbook selection pro-cess might work in your school or district.

In many schools, rather than having each individual teacher select from among a set of available textbooks, a committee is selected to do this work. Therefore, there must be a chairperson and a set of agreed-upon procedures that will be used to come up with a decision.

When you look at the criteria and consider the time that will be required to consider each and every one of them for, say, five textbooks, it's clear that textbook selection is a time-consuming process. Therefore, one way to speed up the process is to have a division of labor on the textbook selection committee.

The division of labor can work in one of two ways. One way is to have each member of the committee take one text and document the extent to which it meets each of the criteria. Another alternative is to have each committee member specialize in one area of review, such as instructional design considerations, and review all of the texts according to the criteria in this category. Either of these two methods is effective. Our preference is for the latter because it gets everyone looking at all the texts, but it does not allow one person's view of one text to unduly influence all of the other committee members.

During its first meeting, the committee should agree on the criteria that will be applied in selecting the text and, perhaps, they might even agree how to weigh the criteria to be used to reach that decision. The committee should then agree upon the actual responsibilities of each committee member and decide how much time should be made available to carry out those responsibilities. After individual review of the texts, committee members should meet again to discuss each of the texts openly and thoroughly, and to come to a consensus decision as to the book or books that will be selected.

Now that we have discussed an overall plan for reviewing texts, the question remains as to how you actually apply the criteria listed in Table 6.1 to evaluate a textbook. This might best be done by using a rating scale of one to five. For example, the first criterion is that the information in the text is accurately stated. If you examine a number of sections in the text and find nothing that is inaccurate, then the text would receive a rating of five. If there is a minor inaccuracy, then the text might receive a rating of four, and so on down the scale. A similar type of rating scale could be used with each criterion.

One of the methods often used in textbook evaluation is that of sampling. Since it is almost impossible to have the time to read every page of every text that is being considered, some type of sampling procedure must be used. The need for sampling is most evident in the first criterion category: the review of the content of the text. Let's review the four major criteria in that category and see how you might assess a text against them.

Content   The first indicator of content accuracy is that the information is factually stated. Here it would probably be best to choose sections in which you have the greatest knowledge of the content and then review those sections in some detail for factual accuracy. Likewise, in determining the extent to which the content is up-to-date, it would be appropriate to select those particular topics in which events have occurred in the past five years. Those events should be reflected in the text. Turn to the topics in the index and see if they are listed. Then review their description in the text to determine their currency and accuracy. The review of the copyright date is done quite easily by referring to the back of the title page in the front of the book.

To determine if the content in the text is comprehensive and congruent with district or state guidelines, it is necessary to do a more complete analysis of the text. In this particular case, you can be quite certain that there will be some overlap between the guidelines and the content of the text; the question is the degree of overlap between the two. Therefore it is necessary to check a large number of items at both the general and specific levels in order to determine the extent of congruence between the text and the curriculum guidelines.

The sampling strategy might be used to test for the social fairness of the text. Many sections of the text can be examined and pictures analyzed to determine whether there is a wide range of ethnic groups and a nearly equal number of males and females represented in the text, and that none are represented in a stereotypic fashion.

Presentation   Sampling is also useful in judging the presentation of information in the text. For example, in checking the format you can examine various chapters to determine if there is only one theme present in each chapter. Then look at the corresponding illustrations to determine if they are appropriate for the learners. It is also sensible to use sampling to conduct an in-depth review of the vocabulary and symbols used in various portions of the text to determine if the vocabulary and symbols are appropriate. The examination of the writing style and the tone that it reflects can also be done for sample sections throughout the text. More specific analysis must be made of the directions and explanations to insure that they are clearly stated.

Instructional design   To examine the instructional design features of a text, you might randomly sample portions of the text dealing with several topics with which you are quite familiar. Determine if a topic is represented by one or more behavioral objectives. Then try to identify the test items that go with that particular objective and determine if the item or items really do measure the objective. Next, find the body of text related to the objective and read it carefully. The critical issue is usually not whether the topic itself is covered, but whether the information is sufficient for the learner to actually learn the skills described in the objective. If it is not sufficient, how much additional instruction must be provided by the instructor?

A similar approach might be employed to look at other instructional design features of a text. For example, does a section you have selected appear to be interesting or motivational for learners? Are practice activities provided, and if so, are they consistent with the skills described in the objectives, as well as with the content preceding the practice activities? At the end of each chapter, are there summaries to bring together all the major ideas? These indicators can all be evaluated on a random sampling basis in order to provide a rating on the instructional design features of the text.

Classroom use   As stated earlier, the most important information you can obtain regarding classroom use of a textbook is data concerning the performance and attitudes of students who previously used it. If this information is not available from the publisher, then perhaps it can be provided by fellow teachers. Information regarding teacher reactions can also be gathered from these sources. Information provided by the publishers or fellow teachers should also be sought to determine if a specific staff development activity or particular physical environment is required to use the text effectively.

If supplementary print materials accompany the text, it is important to sample a large range of these materials to determine the extent to which they are congruent with the content in the text. For example, you might take those areas which you examined when you checked for instructional design features and trace them into the supplemental materials, as well as the teachers' edition, to determine if consistency can be found. Also check the teachers' edition to determine if there are clear suggestions as to how to use the text.

Upon completion of the review of the texts, overall ratings must be developed. If each of the twelve criteria was given a rating from one to five, it would be possible to sum the ratings to obtain a rating for the text. The total score may not be the determining factor, but certainly it should be very important in determining the overall rating for the text. If the committee or individual reviewers think any of the particular criteria are of greater importance than others, then these can be weighted to appropriately influence the total score.

Reviewers may also use these ratings as a vehicle for stimulating discussions among committee members as to the strengths and weaknesses of any textbook. Clearly it will be very difficult for any textbook to receive a perfect rating on every criterion. Therefore, no matter which text is selected, it will have certain weaknesses. These weaknesses should be known to teachers before they use the text so that any supplemental activities that may be required can be planned in advance.

PRACTICE

1. Review the problem scenario at the beginning of this chapter. Assume that you are on the district textbook selection committee that has been asked to select a reading series for grades K–6. How would you suggest that the committee proceed in reaching a decision in a reasonable amount of time?

2. Assume that you have taken a position in which the textbook for the course you are to teach has already been selected. Describe how an examination of that textbook with regard to the criteria stated in Table 6.1 might help you to have a better understanding of the text.

3. Anne Saunders was appointed to the district textbook committee to choose the social studies text for the eighth grade. Her committee chose to ask each committee member to examine a textbook and to report their findings to the committee.

    Anne examined her textbook with regard to the criteria in Table 6.1. Her findings related to each criterion are listed below. As you read Anne's findings, rate the textbook. Use a scale of 1 (lowest) to 5 (highest) to rate the textbook in light of each criterion. When you have finished, add up your ratings and see how they compare with Anne's.

A. Content

1. Accuracy of Content: Found only one minor error of factual content after randomly reviewing 10 percent of the pages in the book. Rating: ———

2. Currency of Content: Examination of the book indicated that several recent events were included and that the book carried this year as its copyright date. Rating: ———

3. Comprehensiveness: When the district curriculum guidelines were compared to the topics in the book, it was found that 15 of the 17 major topics were addressed in the textbook. Rating: ———

4. Social Fairness: Examination of a random sample of 10 percent of the pages in the text indicated that various ethnic groups were broadly represented both in illustrations and the uses of surnames, and that the book contained no stereotyping, particularly with regard to males and females in particular occupations. No particular violation of the social fairness concept was observed in the text. Rating: ———

B. Presentation

5. Text Format: An examination of five of the chapters indicated that each contained only one major theme. In addition, the print size and use of headings was certainly appropriate for the grade level. However, there was a serious problem with the illustrations and photographs in the text. Often they appeared to be simply filler and had little or no relationship to the concepts being taught. Rating: ———

6. Grade Level: A reading of a number of sections of the text indicated that the vocabulary was at approximately the level of the learners and that the readability level of the text was stated by the publisher to be eighth grade. Rating: ———

7. Writing Style: The tone and style of the book seemed to be quite appropriate for the intended learners. However, the directions and explanations for several exercises were not very clear and it was possible to see how the students might have problems trying to decide what to do. Rating: ———

C. Instructional Design

8. Congruency: Having selected six major objectives, the test items examined were found to be perfectly consistent with the behaviors described in those

objectives. In addition, the content for each objective was quite clear and targeted on the objectives. Rating: ———

9. Instructional Characteristics: The case studies that were listed in the text appeared to be very interesting, and there were good practice activities provided in each chapter. However, no end-of-chapter summaries were found in any of the chapters examined. Rating: ———

D. Classroom Use

10. Data Regarding Instructional Effectiveness: There were no data available on the performance of students on test items related to the objectives in the text, nor were there are any indications of student attitudes toward the text. Rating: ———

11. Compatibility with Teaching Conditions: There was nothing to indicate or suggest that any special setting or materials will be necessary to successfully use the text. A statement from the publisher indicated that staff-development activities would be provided for teachers by the publisher if such were requested by the school district. The publisher reported that several teachers who had used the text had been surveyed and they had indicated they were quite satisfied with the quality of the text. Rating: ———

12. Supplementary Print Materials: The teachers' edition was examined for its treatment of the same six objectives examined for criterion number eight. The teachers' edition was consistent with the text and it appeared to be quite helpful in explaining how to help students in understanding the major concepts. Similarly, the workbook activities for the six objectives also were consistent with the content of the text. Rating: ———

FEEDBACK

1. Being on the district reading textbook selection committee would probably require a great deal of time. Rather than reviewing individual texts, your committee would have to review several series of reading texts. Your first task would probably be to select for in-depth review the reading series from about five publishers. This might be done by selecting certain critical criteria, and applying them to all the series first to eliminate those that are least likely to receive a high rating.

   With the task reduced to evaluating five reading series, a decision would have to be made as to what the role of each committee member would be. In this particular case, perhaps two or three committee members would be assigned to each reading series and then each would check from four to six criteria for that particular series.

   Each subcommittee would produce a total rating plus their written assessment of the textbook series. Each text subcommittee would discuss their findings and come to a consensus about their evaluation of the series. These findings would then be presented to the whole group and a final decision made. It would not be entirely unlikely that two or more textbook series would be selected for a district if there were distinctly different types of students in the district and if different series had been designed to meet the needs of each type of student.

2. If a textbook has already been selected, it is still worthwhile to use the criteria to determine what the text is really like. For example, a review of the content to determine its factual accuracy and its currentness is very important to decide whether supplemental materials are needed to bring a text up-to-date. Likewise, it is important to determine the extent to which a text is consistent with the district and state curriculum guidelines, and to determine whether supplemental materials are needed to cover topics not addressed in the text. Determining the social fairness of the text is also important to anticipate any problems once the text is being used by students.

    The overall appearance and format of the text is important to examine to determine whether it is appropriate for the types of learners who would use it. By knowing the vocabulary level, tone, and explicitness of the directions, it is possible to know how to adjust your teaching activities.

    Examining the relationship among the objectives, assessments, and contents helps to determine whether you need to develop your own test items or supplement the text with additional information. For example, knowing that there are insufficient practice activities or summaries helps in designing your particular lessons.

    Detailed examination of a teachers' edition indicates how much help you could receive there and the extent to which the supplemental materials would be helpful to you. Check with the publisher to determine the availability of inservice training for teachers and reactions from teachers and students who have used the text. Knowing the level of student performance and attitudes towards the text when tried out in other districts would be helpful in setting realistic expectations as to what you might be able to achieve, as well as to help you identify the extent to which you need to supplement the text.

    The criteria could be quite useful even when a textbook has already been selected.

3. A. Content
        1. Accuracy of Content: 4
        2. Currency of Content: 5
        3. Comprehensiveness: 4
        4. Social Fairness: 5

    B. Presentation
        5. Text Format: 3
        6. Grade Level: 5
        7. Writing Style: 4

    C. Instructional Design
        8. Congruency: 5
        9. Instructional Characteristics: 4

    D. Classroom Use
        10. Data Regarding Instructional Effectiveness: 1
        11. Compatibility with Teaching Conditions: 5
        12. Supplementary Print Materials: 5
             Total: 50

APPLICATION

Select at least two textbooks that might be used in teaching the goals and objectives in your instructional plan. Review each textbook separately according to at least six, if not all twelve, of the criteria listed in Table 6.1, and indicate your rating of each text on the criteria. Total the criteria and determine which of the two texts would be more appropriate for you to use. Also indicate if any of the criteria should be given additional weight, and for what reason. Apply that weighting to your ratings and see if your textbook selection decision is changed.

SUMMARY

More and more teachers are participating in the selection of textbooks. This process is based upon the establishment of agreed-upon criteria in the areas of content, presentation, instructional design, and classroom use. When these criteria are applied to a set of textbooks, they provide both numeric and qualitative information that can be used to select one or more texts for use in the schools, as well as to identify the strengths and weaknesses of each of the texts. The same criteria can be used to select any supplemental print materials that will be required for use with the text.

CHAPTER SEVEN
DEVELOPING INSTRUCTIONAL ACTIVITIES

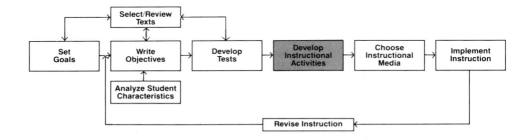

Instructional activities are the result of responsible planning based upon the expectations we have for students as expressed in goals, objectives, and assessments. The availability of a text also influences how we plan the activities that result in students achieving our goals.

PROBLEM SCENARIO

Mary Gallini was more than disappointed. She had just finished scoring the unit test on writing critical essays. A few of her students had done a good job, but many of them had made a wide variety of errors they simply should not have made. Mary thought back to when she had started this topic. There had been so much material to present, and the curriculum guide had not organized it well. So, when she had presented the information on writing skills, she felt as if she were jumping all over the place and not staying on track. The students seemed to have liked the games she inserted into several lessons, but that did not seem to have improved their performance. Mary thought "I have got to get organized." Is there anything that Mary could have done to both reduce her own frustration, and improve the performance of the students?

CHAPTER OBJECTIVES

The objectives for this chapter are that you will be able to

1. describe the major activities in an instructional plan
2. describe the instructional activities for various learning outcomes and types of students
3. develop an instructional plan that is appropriate for given objectives, tests, and types of students

BACKGROUND INFORMATION

If you talk with teachers and observe what they do in the classroom, you will find that some are very effective in their use of lectures, while others like to use discussions to elicit ideas from students. Some teachers are very effective in designing both individual and group practice activities, while others can maintain students' attention by telling stories about their own experiences. Perhaps you already know the types of instructional activities that you feel most confident in using. However, to be an effective teacher you should not focus on any one method to the exclusion or minimization of the others.

Research has suggested that there is a sequence of events that results in the most efficient and effective approach to learning. These events are general steps that can be followed in planning instruction. These events provide an overall instructional strategy, or plan, within which the specific details of a particular lesson are incorporated.

As we talk about an instructional plan, we won't use the terms *unit plan* or *lesson plan*, but it may help you to do so if you have used these terms in the past. We are simply talking about a plan for organizing instruction to teach one or more objectives related to instructional goals. In some districts an instructional plan will be referred to as a lesson plan, in others it will be called a unit plan, and in other districts another label may be applied.

MAJOR CONCEPTS AND EXAMPLES

An instructional plan is a description of what will be presented to students, how it will be presented, and in what sequence. It is essentially a road map for you to use as you plan and implement instruction for a particular instructional goal.

TABLE 7.1. Form for an Instructional Plan

Goal:

Objective(s):

Sample Test Item(s):

INSTRUCTIONAL ACTIVITY	CONTENT OF ACTIVITY	MEANS OF PRESENTING ACTIVITY
1. Motivation		
2. Objectives		
3. Prerequisites		
4. Information and Examples		
5. Practice and Feedback		
6. Testing		
7. Enrichment and Remediation		

THE COMPONENTS OF AN INSTRUCTIONAL PLAN

An instructional plan includes seven instructional activities. These are activities carried out by the teacher (or other instructional media) and students, usually with the aid of a textbook and chalkboard, in order to achieve the instructional goal. As we describe these activities some of them may appear to be very obvious because they are present in all good instruction. However, the activities that we list have emerged from learning research over the last fifty years.

Table 7.1 provides an outline for an instructional plan. Across the top of the outline, there is a place to indicate the goal and objective(s), as well as sample test items, that will be addressed by this plan. Below this area, in the first column, is a list of seven instructional activities. The middle column is labeled "Content of Activity." In this column you briefly describe the substance of each of the activities for your particular lesson. In the right-hand column, labeled "Means of Presenting Activity," you indicate how each activity will actually be presented to the learners. In this chapter and the next, we discuss each of the portions of this outline in detail, and describe how to use the outline to help you develop your instructional plans. Now let's begin by looking at each of the seven instructional activities from Table 7.1 that are listed separately below.

1. Motivation
2. Objectives
3. Prerequisites
4. Information and Examples
5. Practice and Feedback
6. Testing
7. Enrichment and Remediation

Motivation

It is not surprising that research indicates that unless you have the attention of your students, it is very hard to get them to learn. In preparing instruction, however, we sometimes overlook this notion. In such instances, we assume that students are motivated and that we do not have to do anything to gain their attention and maintain that attention throughout instruction. At times, however, this assumption is incorrect; we must plan activities that will motivate our students.

Motivating learners is probably one of the most important issues for the teacher in the classroom. How do we get a "hook" into students in order to maintain their attention? While there are some general approaches to motivating learners, such as the use of reinforcements or token systems, we are more concerned with specific activities related to specific learning outcomes. For example, if you were about to begin a new unit on transportation, you might display bright posters around the room on that day to stimulate student interest in the topic. In other situations you might discuss particular examples that you know are directly related to activities that are going on in students lives and are of immediate importance to them.

Actually, when you consider the area of motivation, there are many kinds of activities that can be undertaken before, during, and following instruction to gain and maintain student interest. These types of activities include arousing student curiosity, making instruction relevant to student interests, and providing rewards for the attainment of objectives. These sorts of activities should be considered and, when appropriate, incorporated into the motivational component of your plan.

Objectives

At a fairly early stage, learners should be informed of what it is that they are going to be able to do when they finish the instructional process. By knowing what will be expected of them, learners may be better able to guide themselves through that process. Indeed, research has shown that in many cases learner performance will be improved if we simply make our objectives explicit before we begin our instruction.

As was discussed in Chapter Three, there are many ways in which we can inform students about our objectives. It is unlikely that you would give them a list of three-component objectives. There may be times when it will not even be necessary to provide anything in writing to students. Simply describing the outcomes of instruction may be sufficient, or you may want to provide examples of what the students will be able to do. Clearly, this second instructional event can be closely related to how to motivate learners if, in fact, they are eager to acquire the skill or knowledge that is to be taught.

Prerequisites

We have already talked about prerequisites as the skills, knowledge, and attitudes students must have in order to begin your instruction. Research has indicated that learning is most effective when we can relate new knowledge and skills to knowledge and skills that we have already learned. If we have the prerequisite knowledge and skills at our disposal, and we are reminded that we already know certain skills, the learning of the new task is often a fairly straightforward matter. New learning is accomplished by building upon what we already know. That is why it is important to help learners recall the necessary prerequisites before you begin to teach them some new skills or knowledge.

On the other hand, if our learners are unable to recall, or have not learned, the necessary prerequisites, it will be very difficult for them to acquire new knowledge. That is why prerequisites are so important and why it is important that a teacher remind students that they already have the skills to begin a new objective. If the teacher finds that most of the students lack the prerequisites, then prior to teaching the new objective, the prerequisites must be taught. If only a few students lack the prerequisites, they can be provided special instruction prior to the unit.

Information and Examples

For most objectives, there is some information that must be presented to the learners, or information that the learners must discover, before they can perform the behavior described in the objective. For example, before most students are able to solve a particular class of problems, such as division problems involving two fractions, they typically are informed of the rule or rules that can be used to solve such problems. Or, if students are learning to analyze the conditions that led to the economic depression in the United States in the 1930s, we must inform them what those conditions were. Similarly, in the case of knowledge objectives, it is obvious that before learners can recall some information, that information must be provided to them. In the case of motor skills, it is necessary to provide learners with a verbal or visual description of the physical process involved in performing a particular skill.

As the examples in the previous paragraph clearly indicate, an important part of the instructional process involves providing learners with necessary information. Although the previous statement may seem quite obvious, in many lessons learners are never provided with the information they need to know.

In addition to providing learners with the necessary information, it is important to give them examples so that they can see how they can use the information. For example, if we provide learners with the rule for solving division problems involving two fractions, it is important that we demonstrate how to solve such problems. Similarly, it is very important to demonstrate motor skills to learners, regardless of whether we provide them with a description of the steps involved in the performance.

Practice and Feedback

In most cases, in order for students to be able to acquire a particular skill, knowledge, or attitude, they must practice that behavior. Therefore, practice activities should be directly related to the skills, knowledge, and attitudes reflected in your objectives. So, for example, if one of your objectives calls for students to be able to write similes, then the most appropriate practice exercise would be to have your students do just that. Your practice activity for this objective would be insufficient if it were limited to the practice of related behaviors, such as identifying similes in given sentences.

After learners have practiced a behavior, it is important for them to receive some feedback. Feedback is the information a learner receives regarding the answer or answers he or she provided. At a minimum, feedback lets the learner know whether an answer was correct. In addition, feedback may indicate what the correct answer was, why it was correct, and, perhaps, what was wrong with the learner's incorrect answer.

Research indicates that providing learners with feedback is a crucial part of the instructional process. Simply having students practice an activity without providing them with any feedback does not necessarily result in effective learning. Indeed, if a student practices the wrong behaviors and is not corrected, that practice activity is likely to be very counter-productive. Thus, when you are developing your instructional plan, you should think about the type of feedback you will provide to students after they complete your practice activities.

Testing

After students have been provided the opportunity to practice the new skill they are learning, there is a point at which testing must be provided to determine the students' ability to perform the new skill. In the chapter on developing tests, we have indicated how important it is that the testing activities be directly related to the behaviors described in the objectives, and we will return again to this theme in Chapter 9. At this point, we simply note that your instructional plan should include a provision for a test, usually administered at the end of the unit of instruction, that assesses the behavior(s) specified in your objective(s). In addition, you may want to plan for some smaller "formative" tests that might be administered during the unit in order to assess student progress toward the attainment of the objectives. This aspect of testing also will be discussed in detail in Chapter Nine.

Enrichment and Remediation

While we would like to think that at the conclusion of a lesson, all of our students will achieve the behaviors that our lesson is designed to teach, this outcome is quite unlikely. There is a much greater likelihood that, at least initially, some of our learners will acquire the behaviors and others will not. Therefore, if we want all our students to master an objective, we must be prepared to provide remedial activities for the unsuccessful learners and enrichment activities for those who are successful. The remedial activities should be directly targeted on the problems demonstrated by the students in the original instruction. The enrichment activities should extend our students' knowledge of a topic or challenge them to apply it in interesting situations. These enrichment activities certainly should not be viewed as punitive, but rather as opportunities for students who are successful to go on to other topics or to do other things that are important to them.

The seven instructional activities we have described comprise an instructional plan. These activities should be considered each time a new instructional goal and a set of instructional objectives are to be presented to students. Research has indicated that all of these activities are important in the learning process. If you doubt this observation, go back to the list and think about omitting one from your instruction and consider the possible consequences. While you may find that the omission of one activity is less critical than the omission of another, all of the activities are important and therefore should be included in an instructional plan.

Instructional Activities and the Domains of Learning

The seven instructional activities are applicable to all four domains of learning (knowledge, intellectual skills, motor skills, and attitudes). However, research has shown that in order to promote effective learning in the various domains, particular activities should be emphasized during your instruction. These activities vary with the domain of learning.

Knowledge objectives   With knowledge objectives, the most important consideration in the information component of the plan is the creation of a larger, more meaningful context for learning that knowledge. For example, if your students have already identified where the states are on the map, it is easier for them to insert the state capitals, as opposed to simply trying to learn the state capitals by memory.

With knowledge objectives, it is also important that you present your students with all the information they will be accountable for, and then have them practice that information extensively. That practice usually consists of writing or verbalizing the knowledge and using it in various ways. Feedback for knowledge objectives usually can consist of simply informing the student of the correct answer, or having the student look up the answer. For example, if some students forget the capital of Georgia, they can easily find that information in their instructional materials.

Intellectual-skills objectives   When we look at the domain of intellectual skills, a number of things become apparent. First, if students do not have the prerequisites necessary to begin instruction on an intellectual-skills objective, it is almost certain that they will be unable to attain that objective. For example, if students do not know how to multiply and subtract, they will be unable to solve long-division problems. Therefore, the establishment of those prerequisites is critical to the success of the instruction.

The use of examples is also very important when you are teaching intellectual skills. In most cases, it will not be sufficient to simply present a set of rules to your students. In addition, you will have to demonstrate the application of those rules so that your students really begin to understand how the rules are to be applied. For example, if you were teaching students how to compute their net worth, you would not only provide the formula, you would also give a number of examples which take different factors into consideration. Some of the factors may not be relevant to net worth. Therefore, using a variety of examples and non-examples (examples that typify mistakes often made in the application of the rules) is extremely important for the acquisition of intellectual skills.

When you are teaching intellectual skills to your students, you should also provide them with sufficient practice and feedback. The use of response-specific feedback is particularly important. Consider a situation in which a student is asked to add $\frac{1}{3} + \frac{1}{3}$ and responds that the answer is $\frac{2}{6}$. In this case, it most likely would not be sufficient to inform the student that the correct answer is $\frac{2}{3}$. Instead, it is important that the student is provided with feedback that is specific to the error. In our example, the student would be told that when two fractions with the same denominator are added together, you do not add the two denominators, instead you simply add the numerators and place the total over the denominator that appeared in both fractions.

In summary, when you are teaching an intellectual skill, several instructional activities should be emphasized. These include ensuring that the students have the necessary prerequisites, demonstrating the application of the skill through a variety of examples, and providing the students with sufficient practice and response-specific feedback.

Motor-skills objectives   Consider now an instructional plan for teaching a motor skill. You may combine several instructional activities when you are teaching motor skills to your students. For example, if an instructor explains and demonstrates a motor skill to the students, this may be considered as motivation for the learners (inasmuch as they would like to do what they have seen done), informing them of what the objectives of the instruction are, and providing them with the information and examples necessary to perform the skill.

Before students can perform a motor skill, they must know the "executive routine," or series of steps, that must be followed in the process of performing the skill. When we provide our learners with this knowledge, we may either think of it as providing them with the necessary prerequisites, or providing them with the essential instructional information. We prefer the latter designation. However, no matter what we call the activity, usually it is important that part of our instructional strategy for teaching motor skills involves providing our students with a verbal description of the executive routine.

After students have learned the executive routine for a motor skill, then practice and feedback become critical. In many situations, the students might begin by practicing the components that make up the skill and then practice integrating those components into a smooth motor performance. As for feedback, with some motor skills the execution of the act itself provides sufficient feedback to indicate to students whether they performed the skill correctly. Archery is an example. However, in other situations like swimming, students must be observed by the teacher, who can tell them what is right or wrong.

Attitude objectives   In developing an instructional plan for an attitude, two instructional activities are extremely important. The first activity is motivation. Determining ways in which to gain or maintain students' attention in the instruction, while always important, is particularly critical when you are working on attitude objectives. It is unlikely that we will be able to have our learners acquire new attitudes if we cannot convince them of the value of incorporating those attitudes into their own value system.

When it comes to attitude teaching, the second important instructional activity is presenting students with information about the attitude. Research has indicated that a successful way of shaping attitudes is to have someone whom your learners admire demonstrate the behavior you want them to acquire. We often see this technique employed in television commercials in which the advertiser attempts to influence our thinking by having people we admire advocate the use of certain products or advocate not participating in particular kinds of activities. In summary, when you are developing an instructional strategy for teaching attitudes, motivational activities and the presentation of information by someone recognized and admired by your students are very important considerations.

The most important features of instructional plans for skills in the four domains are summarized in the chart "Critical Instructional Activities by Learning Domain." While these are the most important activities, it is assumed that many others, which are not stressed, will still be provided.

CRITICAL INSTRUCTIONAL ACTIVITIES BY LEARNING DOMAIN

Domain	Activities
Knowledge	Create context, provide sufficient practice
Intellectual Skills	Stress prerequisites, examples, practice with feedback
Motor Skills	Provide executive routine, practice with feedback
Attitudes	Motivate students to change, provide information on how to change

Instructional Plans for Different Types of Students

It is of interest to examine instructional activities with regard to the different types of learners that we have discussed in previous chapters. How does an instructional plan vary for below-average, average, and above-average students? In the case of below-average learners, we have indicated that often we have to break objectives down into smaller objectives to have the instruction more nearly fit their ability to learn in the classroom. In addition, as we look at various instructional activities we can see that with below-average learners, it is even more important to increase your emphasis upon motivation and make sure that the learners have the necessary prerequisite knowledge. Furthermore, a common observation of those who teach these students is that they often forget the knowledge that they have seemingly acquired. Therefore, prior to new instruction, such students frequently must be reminded of what they have already learned.

In working with below-average learners, it also is important to use a large number of examples. Similarly, the use of a lot of practice and feedback in which they experience success is critically important, as is the use of frequent testing over small segments of instruction. Finally, with below-average learners it is particularly important to plan for remedial activities. If, through the use of remedial activities, you can insure that your students attain one set of objectives before you proceed with instruction on the next set, then it will be less likely that your learners will experience "cumulative failure"—the building of failure upon failure that often occurs with below-average learners.

In contrast to the approach taken with below-average learners, it is often possible with above-average students to actually omit some of the activities in an instructional plan. For example, you may find that these learners are extremely motivated to learn the objectives and therefore no special effort to motivate them is necessary. There also may be little concern with informing them of the prerequisites because we are certain they already have them. Also, because of the ability of these students to grasp ideas rapidly, the number of examples and non-examples you present may be reduced, as may the amount of practice and feedback you provide. Therefore, in developing a strategy for above-average students, it is important to recognize the abilities and knowledge that they bring to the learning situation and not create inefficient instruction that bores them.

When we consider average learners, the events of instruction seem to be made for them. With such learners, the emphasis we place upon each instructional event is likely to be influenced much more heavily by the type of learning outcome we are working with, rather than the type of learner. After we have tried out our instructional plan with our students, regardless of their special characteristics, we may choose to modify it. How to decide upon such modifications will be discussed in Chapter Ten.

✳ Developing an Instructional Plan

Let's look at two examples of how you might go about developing an instructional plan. In the first example, the instructional goal is to have students be able to solve mathematical word problems. The specific objective is to have students be able to solve written problems that involve rate, time, and distance by correctly using the formula $D = R \times T$.

The first step is to identify that this objective is an intellectual skill, and involves rule using. Because it is an intellectual skill, we need to emphasize the availability of prerequisite skills, provide a variety of examples, and have available a number of practice and feedback activities. We will assume that this instruction is being prepared for average seventh graders. There will be no special variations in the instructional plan to accommodate the characteristics of these students. With this information in mind, you might develop the following set of instructional activities. Please note that we have described the plan in some detail. If we were simply preparing it for our own use, we would be likely to use one or two sentences to summarize our plan for each instructional activity, and we would list this information in the "content" column of the form displayed in Table 7.1.

1. *Motivation.* Remind students that the speed limits on the highways in our state have recently increased. If we take a trip elsewhere in our state (to relatives,

friends, recreation areas, for example) it will take less time to get there if we travel at the speed limit. How can we figure out how much time it will take?

2. *Objective.* Tell the students that the objective is to be able to solve problems in which they have to figure how far, how fast, or how long it will take to travel, given written information about two of these factors. They will use a mathematical formula to do this.

3. *Prerequisites.* We know that the students have the basic math skills (add, subtract, multiply, and divide), that they comprehend the concept of travel and movement from one point to another, and we remind them that they know that movement requires time. Perhaps the most critical prerequisite is understanding how a formula like $D = R \times T$ is used to determine an unknown component within that formula. Perhaps reviewing a similar formula that the students have already used would be appropriate.

4. *Information and Examples.* Distance = Rate × Time ($D = R \times T$). Explain each concept: rate, time, and distance. Provide numerous examples, first using the easiest situation, in which rate and time are multiplied in order to determine distance. Then move to examples in which rate equals distance divided by time, and time equals distance divided by rate. Present each example in the context of a word problem involving (a) traveling in a car, train, plane, or boat, or (b) running or walking.

5. *Practice and Feedback.* Provide students with a set of ten problems that vary in terms of whether the students have to solve for time, rate, or distance. For variety in instructional approach, and in order to have the students help each other, organize the students into teams and give them thirty minutes to solve the problems. Afterwards, review the problems in detail with the entire class and explain the correct answers. If overall performance is poor, review the information with new examples and give additional practice problems for students to work on individually. With this approach, it will be possible to identify exactly which students are still having problems.

6. *Testing.* Administer a fifteen-item test to all students (to be taken individually, not in teams). The test will consist of five items in which distance is computed given rate and time, five items in which the rate is computed given time and distance, and five problems in which time is computed given rate and distance.

7. *Enrichment and Remediation.* Based on their scores on the test, students would either be given enrichment or remedial activities in this particular situation. The enrichment activity for those students who did very well would be to serve as tutors for those students who did not. The students receiving remediation would be given additional problems to solve in conjunction with their tutor. Based upon examination of the kinds of problems experienced on the test, additional remediation may be provided.

Table 7.2 shows how this strategy would look using the outline we have suggested you employ.

It should be noted that the instructional plan presented here is just one of many possible plans for teaching a procedure for solving mathematical word problems. In addition, please note that there are still a number of decisions to be made with regard to the strategy. For example, we must decide upon what media, if any, will be incorporated into the presentation of the instruction. We also have to develop the actual work-

TABLE 7.2. Instructional Plan

Goal: Solve mathematical word problems.

Objective(s): Solve word problems that involve rate, time, and distance by using the formula
$D = R \times T$.

Sample Test Item(s): Walter has been running for thirty minutes at seven miles per hour. How much distance has he covered?

INSTRUCTIONAL ACTIVITY	CONTENT OF ACTIVITY	MEANS OF PRESENTING ACTIVITY
1. Motivation	Use highway travel and new speed limits.	
2. Objective	Tell students they will solve word problems involving how far, fast, and long it takes to travel.	
3. Prerequisites	Assume math, travel. Remind that travel takes time, and how to use algebraic equation.	
4. Information and Examples	Explain concepts of rate, time, and distance. Explain formula $D = R \times T$.	
	Give examples using each part of formula as the unknown.	
5. Practice and Feedback	Group students to work on variety of written problems.	
	Review results with class, before individual practice.	
6. Testing	Give a fifteen-item test, consisting of five problems solving for rate, time, and distance.	
7. Enrichment and Remediation	Pair students who mastered the objective with those who did not. Students who mastered serve as tutors for those who did not.	

sheets and tests we will use, and we must determine the roles the teacher and the textbook will play with regard to this topic. Exact classroom procedures will also have to be worked out, although a number of them are suggested in the activities. All of these additional questions will be addressed in the chapters that follow. Our efforts at this point have been devoted to describing briefly the substance or content of our instructional plan, where we have been focusing upon each of the seven major instructional activities.

Our next example deals with the goal of having students be able to critically evaluate foreign-policy positions taken by the United States government. This is part of a senior high school advanced placement social studies course. The students in the course are considered to be college-bound advanced students. The specific objective that they will be working on is to be able to evaluate the U.S. position on nuclear disarmament. As you look at the instructional plan, please note that in light of the characteristics of the students and the topic, we have decided to use a very straightforward method of informing the students of the objective.

1. *Motivation.* Select news articles and editorials that contrast the various sides to this issue. Try to draw out the long-term implications of decisions that will be made in the next few years.

2. *Objectives.* Inform students of the objective for the lesson.

3. *Prerequisites.* When we take a lesson such as this out of context, it is difficult to know exactly what prerequisite skills are necessary. However, it might be appropriate to help the students recall the historical context of the nuclear arms race. It may also be appropriate to review world geography, specifically focusing on the relative location of the United States, the Soviet Union, and Europe.

4. *Information and Examples.* The most important information for this objective is the State Department's policy on nuclear disarmament. This will be presented in a very factual manner. The crucial skills to be learned are how to analyze that policy and to evaluate its effects. Therefore a presentation on policy analysis would be helpful, along with suggestions as to where reactions to the United States policy might be found. One analysis of the disarmament policy might be presented for the students to understand the general nature of the evaluation they are to make.

5. *Practice and Feedback.* The practice on this particular skill would be identifying the relevant arguments, pro and con, regarding this particular policy. This could be done through the examination of the positions by scholars from various countries, and through logical analysis by the students. The information the students gather might be presented in class, with students given the opportunity to debate the pro and con positions with regard to the policy.

6. *Testing.* Perhaps the best test of this objective would be for the teacher to propose an amendment to the present policy that would change it in a significant fashion. Students would be asked to analyze the consequences of this amendment to the policy and to express their support of the position they take.

7. *Enrichment and Remediation.* Based upon the analysis of the test, it may be determined that none of the students really need any remedial activity. For enrichment, they might examine the Soviet Union's policy on nuclear disarmament and conduct a similar type of analysis.

The information presented for each activity would be incorporated into an instructional plan like those shown in Tables 7.1 and 7.2. Note again that the instructional plan for this objective focuses primarily, but not exclusively, on the content to be covered in the study of this objective. It does not address the role of the textbook or other media, nor does it deal in great detail with the classroom procedures that would be employed.

Before doing the practice activities, you might review the problem scenario for this chapter. If Mary had worked out an instructional plan in which the proper activities were included and appropriately sequenced, it is unlikely that she would have had the problems that were described in the scenario.

PRACTICE

1. Listed below are the labels for the seven instructional activities that are included in an instructional plan. Indicate your understanding of these events by briefly describing each one.
    A. Motivation
    B. Objectives
    C. Prerequisites
    D. Information and Examples
    E. Practice and Feedback
    F. Testing
    G. Enrichment and Remediation

2. Listed below are the four major domains of instructional goals and learning outcomes for students. After each goal, list the instructional events that would receive special consideration if you were teaching an objective in that domain.
    A. Knowledge
    B. Intellectual Skills
    C. Motor Skills
    D. Attitude

3. Listed below are some typical comments that might be heard from students during or after studying a particular topic. Based upon each comment, decide which instructional activity may have been missing from the instructional plan used by the teacher. For example, if a student said "I studied and studied, but I never really understood what it was I was supposed to be learning," we would imagine that the student did not understand what the objective of the lesson was. Apparently, the teacher had not made the objective clear to the student. Now, look at each of the comments below, and decide what instructional event may have been missing.
    A. "I turned in my answers to the homework problems he gave us, but I never found out how well I did."
    B. "I have no idea why we are studying this topic. It doesn't seem to have anything to do with anything I'm interested in."
    C. "We've moved on to Unit three and I still don't understand the stuff from Unit two!"
    D. "We spent a lot of time working on some activities, but I was never clear about exactly what the formula was that we were supposed to be applying. If he had just shown us how to use the formula, maybe I could have done better."
    E. "We go from lesson to lesson to lesson, but we never find out if we are really mastering what we're supposed to be learning. I'm really concerned about what's going to happen at the end of the year if we have a comprehensive final exam."

F.   "I listened as closely as I could to what the teacher said in class, but I didn't understand what she was talking about. I seem to be missing something that I should know to understand this topic."

G.   "I thought we were going to be able to use our textbook when we had to answer those questions. When I got to class I found out we had to do it from memory."

4.   Listed below is a goal and an objective, which is intended for all fourth grade students—below average, average and above average. Develop an instructional plan for achieving this objective by indicating what you would do for each of the seven major instructional activities.
Goal: Practice safety habits at home and school.
Objective: Students choose to practice safe bicycle riding at all times.

You may find this a little difficult, but it brings out some important points, so go ahead and give it a try.

FEEDBACK

1.   Check the appropriate section of this chapter for the answers to this question.
2.   Check the appropriate section of this chapter for the answers to this question.
3.   Activities that were probably omitted from the instructional plan:

A.   Feedback for the practice

B.   Motivation

C.   Remediation or prerequisites

D.   Information and examples

E.   Practice and feedback, or testing

F.   Prerequisites

G.   Conditions for the objective

4.   This is an interesting objective for a number of reasons. First of all, we hope you recognized that it is in the attitudinal domain and therefore we will be particularly concerned about the motivation of the students and the way in which we present the information to them. Secondly, the plan must apply to all fourth graders, below average, average, and above average. It is not clear whether these ability levels are relevant to the teaching of an attitude since they are based primarily upon the students' intellectual skills, not their attitudes. The instructional plan described below was developed with these thoughts in mind. Of course, the activities we propose are just one of many possible sets for teaching this objective. The plan you developed may be quite different, but still may be very appropriate.

1.   *Motivation.* While it may be possible to point out the seriousness of injuries due to careless bicycle riding habits, there probably are more positive ways to show the benefits of safe riding. Having the fourth graders organize a school-wide campaign to promote safe riding might be a good source of motivation.

2.   *Objectives.* We would indicate to the students that we want them to choose to ride their bicycles safely in a variety of riding situations. They might be provided pictures of such situations.

3. *Prerequisites.* Can we assume that all fourth graders have bicycles and can ride a bike? This poses a problem, as does getting the students to bring their bicycles to school. Those who ride the bus will obviously have difficulties. Therefore, this objective might come later in the year, and have as its prerequisite that the students are able to ride a bicycle. Students who do not know how may be taught this skill in their physical education class.

4. *Information and Examples.* Select a role model admired by the students, such as a well-known older student, or someone from the community. Have this person come in and talk to the students and demonstrate the rules for safely riding a bicycle. An important aspect of this event is to point out the major rules and describe instances in which those rules would be important.

5. *Practice and Feedback.* Give students the opportunity to ride the bicycles on the school grounds in situations that simulate problems they might encounter riding to and from school. Teachers and fellow students will provide the children with feedback regarding unsafe practices.

6. *Testing.* Present students with two or three problem situations and ask them to *demonstrate* how they would ride their bicycle in the safest possible fashion in each situation. It should be noted that this is not a true test of our objective because we are not observing the students riding to or from school or at home, but only in a simulation. This is a major problem with the assessment of nearly any attitudinal objective. However, perhaps our assessment activity can include the enrichment activity described below.

7. *Enrichment and Remediation.* For those students who fail in the testing situation, additional instruction may take place based on the kinds of errors that they make. When these errors have been remediated, then, as an enrichment activity for all of the students, a bicycle outing could be planned in which they would be able to demonstrate their knowledge of safe bicycle riding.

APPLICATION

Choose two of the objectives you have written. Make sure they are from two different learning domains. For each objective, develop an instructional plan in the format shown in Table 7.2. Be able to explain your rationale for each of the instructional activities in your plan.

SUMMARY

In this chapter we noted that while not all learning is the same, seven basic activities are common to most learning situations. Those activities are motivation, objectives, prerequisites, information and examples, practice and feedback, testing, and enrichment and remediation. While these activities apply to all of the domains, we noted that certain ones are more important in one domain than another, or take on different characteristics depending on the domain. For example, numerous examples are required when teaching intellectual skills, while in teaching attitudes, the person who presents the instruction is often as important as what is said. It was also noted that an instructional plan may be amplified or abridged based on whether the instruction is being prepared for below-average, average, or above-average learners. Regardless of which activities are emphasized, it is critically important that the overall instructional plan be directed toward enabling learners to attain a particular objective or objectives. In other words, there must be an alignment, or close relationship, between your instructional activities, your objectives, and your assessment.

CHAPTER EIGHT
CHOOSING
INSTRUCTIONAL MEDIA

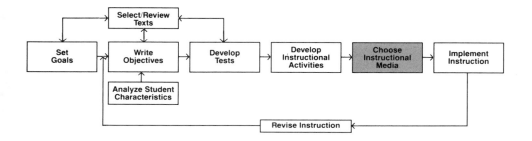

In Chapter Six we focused on one of the two most frequently used means for presenting instruction—the textbook. The teacher, of course, is the other. Indeed, most instruction presented in schools today is delivered by one or the other.

As you go about planning your instruction, it is quite likely that you, too, will rely primarily on yourself and a textbook for presenting instructional content. However, there are likely to be instances when you will want to use other instructional media as part of your instructional plan. How will you decide whether a particular medium is appropriate? That is the question we will focus upon in this chapter.

PROBLEM SCENARIO

Ms. Washington, a fifth grade teacher, has just received a brochure about a new computer software program entitled "Capital Ideas." According to the brochure, "'Capital Ideas' is a drill-and-practice program that will make learning the names of state capitals fun! Students are given the names of states and are asked to name the capitals of each one. Each time a student answers correctly, a state flag appears on the dome of a state capitol. After ten correct responses, a simulated fireworks display appears above the dome."

Ms. Washington's students are supposed to learn the names of the state capitals. She wonders whether she should use "Capital Ideas" to help them.

CHAPTER OBJECTIVES

The objectives for this chapter are that you will be able to

1. identify the questions you should ask when deciding to use an instructional medium
2. identify whether specific media are appropriate for use in a given instructional situation, and provide a rationale for your answer

BACKGROUND INFORMATION

When you hear, or read, the term *instructional media*, what do you think of? Many people would say that they think of such things as films, or filmstrips, or overhead projectors. Others, particularly those who have recently been in school settings, are more likely to mention the computer. All of these things are examples of instructional media.

We would like to define instructional media as the physical means (other than the teacher, textbook, and supplementary print materials) by which instruction is delivered to students. We are excluding the teacher, textbook, and supplementary print materials (such as workbooks) from our definition to distinguish between these traditional means of instruction and the less traditional instructional media we will be focusing on in this chapter.

It is also important to distinguish between media hardware and media software. Media hardware refers to equipment, such as computers, televisions, and tape players. Media software, or mediated materials, are the instructional materials that are presented by means of a piece of media hardware. Examples of mediated materials are computer disks, videocassettes, and records.

MAJOR CONCEPTS AND EXAMPLES

The instructional media we will be discussing in this chapter are less traditional in the sense that teachers, textbooks, and supplementary print materials are used more frequently as a means of presenting instructional activities to students. Indeed, it is likely that when you choose a means for presenting an instructional activity, you will assume that you will present the activity yourself or that you will use a textbook or supplementary print material to do so. However, there are likely to be instances when you may want to incorporate a particular medium in your instructional plan. Under such circumstances, we suggest you ask yourself these three questions.

Is the instructional medium you are considering:

1. practical?
2. appropriate for your students?
3. well-suited to present a particular instructional activity?

Practicality

The question of whether a medium is practical must be examined in terms of the mediated materials (software) you want to use and the media equipment (hardware) that will be required. When it comes to software, do not be surprised if the school you work in does not have many of the computer software packages, instructional videotapes, and other mediated materials of which you may be aware. If they are not readily available, what will be the time and cost involved in obtaining or producing them, and are the administrators at your school likely to approve of the expense?

Even if the desired mediated materials are easily obtainable, there are a number of questions pertaining to media hardware that you should consider. These include the following:

- Is the necessary media hardware (equipment) readily available to you?
- If the hardware is available, can that hardware be easily used in the instructional environment in which you are working?
- If the necessary hardware is not readily available, what will be the time and cost involved in obtaining it, and will the school administrators approve of the expense?

Student Characteristics

When you are thinking about using an instructional medium, it is important for you to consider whether that medium is appropriate for your students. One factor you should take into consideration is the attitudes your students have regarding a particular medium. For example, if you show them an instructional television program, will they be inclined to think of the program as entertainment? If so, how will their perceptions affect their learning?

It is also important to consider your students' knowledge and skills in a particular area. What do your students already know about the content an instructional medium deals with? What content-related skills do your students already possess? In light of the answers to these questions, do you think that the instructional medium presents the content at a level that your students will be able to understand?

Also think about the general abilities of your students. If you are working with below-average learners, then it is likely that most of them will not be good readers. If that is the case, you should consider using non-print media whenever appropriate. For example, if you were attempting to teach below-average learners how an automobile engine operates, the description of the process might best be presented by a medium that allows the learners to see and hear how the process works, rather than a medium that requires them to read about the process.

Instructional Activities

The question of whether a particular instructional medium should be used should also be examined in light of the instructional activity it is intended to present. Media differ with respect to their ability to present particular instructional activities. For example, when it comes to presenting information and providing examples, some media are capable of depicting motion and sound, and other media are not. So, if we are interested in describing, in words, how a steam engine operates, almost any medium can do the job. If, however, we are interested in accurately depicting how a steam engine works, our choice of media becomes much more limited; film or television might be the media of choice, since both can accurately depict motion and present sounds.

In addition to differing in their ability to present information and provide examples, media often differ in the ways in which they can present other instructional activities. Let's look at each type of instructional activity and see how various media might be used to support it.

Motivation   As we indicated earlier, media are often used to help present this instructional event. Many teachers have found that they can gain their students' attention by presenting them with interesting visual images ranging from simple black-and-white hand-drawn cartoons to life-like images incorporating motion and color. A variety of media, such as motion pictures, filmstrips, television, computers, slides, charts, and transparencies can be used to present these images.

You may also gain your students' attention or arouse their curiosity by having them listen to various sounds, ranging from the sound of a famous person giving a speech to the sound of the wind during a huricane. In order to present your learners with sounds such as these, a variety of media may be employed, including audio recording (on tapes, discs, or records), television, motion pictures, and slides synchronized with tapes.

Objectives   Teachers often will present their objectives to students orally and/or in writing, via handouts, the chalkboard, or overhead transparencies. However, other media may also be employed for this purpose. For example, if most of the other instructional activities are to be delivered by a particular medium (for example, the computer), then it may be convenient to use that same medium to present your objectives.

Prerequisites   When you are reminding students of the prerequisites they need to recall, an oral statement will often suffice. However, a written reminder of the prerequisites may also be helpful. Such a reminder might be presented via the chalkboard, an overhead transparency, or a written handout.

Information and examples   The media you use in order to present information and examples to your students will depend, in large part, on the nature of the learning outcome you want your students to attain. Let's look at each type of outcome separately.

If your outcome falls in the knowledge domain, then it is important that you present that information to your students within a larger, more meaningful context. Media that can present visual images will often help. For example, rather than merely describing the physical characteristics of Abraham Lincoln to your students, it would be more effective to accompany such a description with pictures of the man. And, inasmuch as sounds may also broaden the context in which facts are presented, then media that present sounds to your learners may also help them to recall certain facts.

In the intellectual skills domain, a large number of outcomes require students to be able to identify different objects based upon their physical characteristics. This is one type of concept learning. An example would be having a student classify various plants based upon each plant's physical features. In order to present students with the information and examples necessary to make such classifications, visual media, such as slides or motion pictures, are often required.

Another type of outcome in the intellectual skills domain requires students to be able to describe the relationship among various things, events, or people (such as the familial relationship between an aunt and her niece). For outcomes of this sort, the use of charts, slides, or other media that can depict the relationship between abstract concepts is particularly important.

Other major outcomes in the intellectual skills domain involve rule-using and problem-solving. Often the printed word is the best way of communicating the information and explaining the examples students need in order to be able to perform these sorts of skills.

In the motor skills domain, the instructional activity called "information and examples" often consists of a live explanation and demonstration. However, media such as motion pictures and television (videotape or videodisk) are particularly good media choices here in that both media possess motion, slow-motion, and stop-action capabilities. Other visual media, such as filmstrips and slides, can also be used for demonstrating motor skills, but their value is diminished somewhat by the fact that these media cannot depict motion.

Finally, in the attitude domain, it is quite valuable to have a person your students admire advocate a view or model a behavior you would like to see your students adopt. In many instances (particularly in the early grades), you the teacher will serve as the role model. On other occasions, respected individuals can be brought into the classroom, but more often than not, you will have to use other means in order to present such individuals to your students. For example, a videotape can be used to present a rock star speaking out against drug use.

In trying to convince students to adopt a particular point of view, messages presented via television or motion pictures may be most effective, inasmuch as these media are usually more capable than others in providing your students with a sense of reality, of being there. Certainly other media, such as audio recordings or slides with tapes, can effectively be used to present information or examples related to attitudes; however, since the former cannot present visual images and the latter cannot depict motion, they may not be as effective as television or motion pictures.

Now that we have discussed some media you might use when you are presenting information and examples to your students, let's turn to the next type of instructional activity.

Practice and feedback   The media you use to present your practice activities should be capable of providing the same conditions as described in your objective. For example, if your objective calls for your students to name various public officials when shown pictures of those officials, then the medium you use during your practice activity should be capable of presenting pictures.

Although some objectives may require that students respond to some pictures or sounds, many more objectives require that students respond to written questions. Therefore, many practice exercises will be presented via worksheets, chalkboards, or computers.

The computer is a particularly good medium for providing practice, especially for intellectual skills. The computer can easily provide an extensive variety of practice problems and, more importantly, adjust the amount, sequence, and difficulty of those problems in light of the student's performance.

Media differ with regard to their capability to provide feedback to students. Whereas some media can "judge" a student's response and provide response-specific feedback, other media usually only provide general feedback. This difference becomes particularly important when you are teaching intellectual skills or motor skills. When your students are practicing these skills, it is important that they receive response-specific feedback that not only indicates whether a response was correct or incorrect, but also provides information designed to help them correct any errors.

For intellectual skills outcomes, computers and interactive videodisks can serve as excellent sources of response-specific feedback. The latter medium can be particularly effective in depicting a real-life problem-solving situation (such as teaching a child how to deal with a bully), asking the viewer to choose from one of several ways to respond to the situation, and then presenting the probable consequences of responding in that fashion.

Most media (other than very expensive simulators) are not capable of providing learners with feedback that appraises the quality of the performance of a motor skill. With such skills, having an instructor observe and critique a student's motor-skill performance is the best means of providing response-specific feedback.

Testing   As is the case with practice exercises, the medium you use to present your test items should be capable of providing the same conditions as those described in your objectives. Similarly, the medium you use to present your test must be capable of "accepting" the types of behaviors specified in your objectives. For example, if one of your objectives calls for the students to demonstrate the procedures for conducting cardiopulmonary resuscitation (CPR), then a paper-and-pencil test, which would merely allow your students to describe CPR procedures, would not be appropriate.

Enrichment and remediation   If the nature of your remedial or enrichment activities permits you to choose from among several appropriate media, then you might want to choose a medium other than those you previously employed as part of your instructional strategy. For example, if you provided your students with a lecture and text material that described the causes of the American Civil War, then you may want to employ a different medium, (like a film) for remediation. Of course, it is quite possible that the students' initial failure was due to problems other than the media you chose. However, choosing another medium to present the remedial instruction may be an appropriate course of action.

Why should you also consider presenting your enrichment activities in a medium other than those used in earlier parts of your instructional strategy? Simply because such a decision would provide your learners with a change of pace they might enjoy.

Preparing Your Own Mediated Materials

Ideally, when you are preparing an instructional plan, all of the materials you need will be readily available. Between the textbook, your own notes, and various mediated materials, you should be able to provide for all of the instructional activities you have planned. However, when you lay out an instructional plan on a step-by-step basis, it often becomes clear that certain instructional activities are not covered by available materials and can not easily be covered by a lecture or discussion. Therefore, there will be times when it will be incumbent upon you to prepare meaningful materials. In this section, we will consider some of the techniques that you can use.

Let's consider the three basic approaches a teacher can take to prepare special materials. These alternatives include writing, drawing, and creating.

Writing Teachers often prepare written materials for their students. Tests are perhaps the most common form of written materials that teachers construct, but there may also be a need for outlines or specific examples that are not available in a textbook. In some cases, it may even be necessary to prepare written materials that present the actual instructional information that must be presented to the students; for example, the rule for converting from kilometers to miles. However, it is more likely that you will need to prepare written materials that provide practice activities for your students. Thus, the written materials you prepare are likely to be in the form of worksheets or game materials.

Once the written materials have been prepared, they can be duplicated and distributed to the students in several basic ways. Certainly the most common of all is the ditto form. In more affluent situations, teachers may have access, on a limited basis, to a photocopying machine. In addition, anything that is written can be copied onto a transparency, and it is not uncommon to find teachers making extensive use of overhead projectors in the classroom.

Drawing For those teachers with sufficient talent, it is quite possible to prepare instructional materials such as diagrams, illustrations, and models in written form. Such materials are developed to provide students with examples of the concepts, rules, or motor skills they are learning. These materials can be duplicated for students or simply displayed on posters, large charts, or bulletin boards for all the students to see.

Creating In some situations, it is possible for teachers to use physical materials in order to create instructional materials. The materials that are created serve as examples of the products teachers want their students to create or become familiar with. For example, we can think of an elementary school teacher who prepares sample food items from a country his students are learning about, or an industrial arts teacher who prepares a sample of a wood product she would like her students to create.

Materials that teachers create can also serve other instructional functions. For example, a teacher might create some manipulative materials that could be used to help teach students mathematical concepts. The teacher could use these materials to help demonstrate concepts, and the students could use the materials to help solve practice exercises. Or a teacher might use audio tapes to present students with stories, compositions, or music that she would like them to hear.

In addition to the low-tech materials typically produced by the techniques described in this section, teachers may choose to produce such high-tech materials as televised or computer-assisted instruction. However, before you choose to produce any type of instructional material, we suggest you think about whether the materials will be (a) practical to use and produce, (b) appropriate for your students, and (c) well-suited to present a particular instructional activity.

Choosing Media: An Example

We have discussed the three factors (practicality, student characteristics, and instructional activities) that you should consider before you decide to use a particular instructional medium. Now let's look at an example of how those factors might come into play.

Ms. Washington, the teacher we discussed in the problem scenario at the beginning of this chapter, is still wondering whether to use "Capital Ideas," the computer software program she read about. She thinks it might serve as a good means of providing her students with practice in learning the state capitals, but before she incorporates it into her instructional plan, she decides to consider it in terms of the three factors we have discussed in this chapter.

First, Ms. Washington examines whether it will be practical to use "Capital Ideas." Although her school does not own the program, the media center director informs Ms. Washington that the district media depository has several copies of the program and that it will be fairly easy to borrow those copies for a week. Another practical concern is that Ms. Washington's classroom is not equipped with any computers. However, the children in her class have access to the computers in the media center twice each week. Ms. Washington decides that during the week they are learning about state capitals, each child will have a sufficient opportunity to use the computer program. Thus, from a practical standpoint, "Capital Ideas" appears to be an appropriate instructional tool.

Second, Ms. Washington considers whether "Capital Ideas" is appropriate in light of characteristics of the children in her class. The children have worked with instructional software before and seemed to have enjoyed doing so. Furthermore, they seem to have learned the content the software programs were designed to help teach. However, Ms. Washington wonders whether this particular software program is appropriate in light of the skills, knowledge, and general ability level of her students. She decides she will preview the program before she makes any decision regarding this issue.

Third, Ms. Washington considers whether "Capital Ideas" is well suited to provide her students with practice in learning the state capitals. She knows that, in general, the computer can serve as a good means of providing students with practice, and the brochure she received about "Capital Ideas" indicates that the program is appropriate for that purpose. Nonetheless, she decides that when she previews the program, she will check to make sure it really will provide her students with the practice they need.

Having considered the three factors described above, Ms. Washington decides that she is likely to use "Capital Ideas" as part of her instructional plan for teaching her students the names of the state capitals. But she wisely decides to preview the program before she makes a final decision.

Computers in Instruction

Before we present you with some practice exercises, we would like to briefly discuss one instructional medium that seems to be getting a great deal of attention—the computer. One of the reasons computers seem to be so popular may be because they are a relatively new educational tool. However, with rare exception, the novelty of computers should not be reason enough to employ them. Instead, we hope that before you decide to use the computer to present a particular instructional activity, you will consider the three factors (practicality, student characteristics, and instructional activities) we have been discussing in this chapter.

The question of practicality is important because in many schools, students have rather limited access to computers. In such situations, you must carefully consider scheduling so that students have access to the computer at the appropriate point in your instructional plan.

Is the computer likely to be an appropriate medium for your students in light of their characteristics? We have found that in most instances, students enjoy working with computers; they usually have little or no fear of the hardware. The crucial issue then becomes whether a particular software program is appropriate for your students in light of their skills, knowledge, and general ability.

The question of whether the computer is well suited to present a particular instructional activity can be examined both in terms of the capabilities of the computer itself (the hardware) and the characteristics of the instructional program (software). With regard to hardware, the computer is a medium that can do a good job of presenting a variety of instructional activities. By being able to present games, colorful graphics, and a variety of encouraging messages to students, it can often be used as an excellent motivational device. In addition, it can be used to progressively disclose print messages, thus making it a good tool for providing learners with instructional information. Because the computer can pose questions and keep a record of student responses, it can serve as a testing device. It also can adjust the questions it poses to students, using the students' responses as the basis for that adjustment. Thus, it can be an excellent tool for presenting practice activities. And, as we have mentioned before, its ability to judge a student's response and provide the student with specific feedback further enhances its instructional value, especially when it comes to teaching intellectual skills. Yet, in spite of all it can do, the computer should not be viewed as the perfect medium; what it is capable of doing and what it is actually used for are usually two different things.

The instructional role a computer is playing at any particular time is determined by the type of instructional program (software) the computer is presenting at that moment. A variety of classification schemes has been used to categorize instructional software. One popular categorization scheme that is quite useful attempts to classify software into one of four categories, depending upon the primary instructional purpose of the software. These four categories are drill-and-practice programs, tutorial programs, simulations, and instructional games. Let's briefly discuss each of these categories.

Drill-and-practice programs are intended to provide students with the opportunity to practice skills or to rehearse the knowledge previously presented to them. Such programs are not intended to provide the initial information and examples students need to learn, and therefore should not serve as the only instruction. Instead, they should be used to reinforce a skill or information that has been presented to students through some other means.

In addition to providing students with practice, drill-and-practice programs usually present them with feedback regarding their performance. Effective drill-and-practice programs for objectives in the intellectual skills domain provide students with response-specific feedback. Moreover, such programs will take a student's previous responses into account when determining the sequence of questions that will be presented. Unfortunately, most drill-and-practice programs lack many of these features.

Whereas drill-and-practice programs focus on the instructional activity we call practice and feedback, *tutorial programs* focus on providing students with information and examples. Tutorial programs often are intended to serve as the primary means of instruction for a given objective, in that the programs provide students with information and examples that may enable them to acquire a particular skill or knowledge. Tutorials may also provide students with some opportunity to practice the behavior being taught, but the practice activities usually are not as extensive as those provided for by drill-and-practice programs. Although some tutorial programs have been designed or used by themselves for instruction, we have found that many tutorial programs must be used in conjunction with other instructional activities for students to acquire the skills or knowledge the tutorial programs are purported to teach.

Simulations are programs designed to provide learners with a simplified model of some aspect of the world. The simulation not only provides the learner with a model, it also gives the learner the opportunity to interact with that model in a lifelike manner. The results of using the model change as actions are taken by the learner. Thus, the learner has the opportunity to experience, in a safe environment, the likely real world consequences of taking particular actions. For example, a simulation may present a student with a visual of an airplane cockpit and provide her with the opportunity to manipulate the aircraft's controls. As she does so, the program allows the student to experience (through pictures and sound) what would happen to the aircraft as a result of her actions.

Like drill-and-practice exercises, *instructional games* are programs that are designed to provide students with practice in performing a particular skill. Unlike regular drill-and-practice exercises, however, instructional games require the student to perform the skill within the context of a game. For example, one instructional game requires a student to shoot at incoming enemy aircraft, each of which has a simple addition problem written on its fuselage. In order to destroy the enemy aircraft, the student must solve the addition problems. When the student types in a correct answer, an enemy plane is destroyed; an incorrect response results in the destruction of one of the student's defending aircraft. In another game, as a child correctly matches shapes and colors, the child is given the opportunity to create a colorful picture. These are but two examples of the many types of challenges presented by instructional games.

Although many students will enjoy playing the instructional games a computer can present, you should be alert to some possible shortcomings. First, some students may not be motivated by the challenge a game presents. Second, many games do not provide the detailed response-specific feedback necessary to teach intellectual skills. Third, on the poorest of computer games, it is not clear what skills are being taught. They appear only to be academic time-fillers, with no apparent educational value.

PRACTICE

1. Table 8.1 is a copy of the first instructional plan discussed in Chapter Seven. Examine the right-hand column (labeled "Means of Presenting Activity"). As you can see, the teacher who developed the plan has decided that she will serve as the primary means of presenting several of the instructional activities. Most of the other activities will be presented by a textbook, worksheets, or by some of the students in the class. However, in order to motivate

10-15 min. RTL Need to have 7 components. capture Attention
motivation (written plan)

Days-two w-m-w something particip. teaching

TABLE 8.1.   Instructional Plan

Goal: Solve mathematical word problems.

Objective(s):   Solve word problems that involve rate, time, and distance by using the formula
$D = R \times T$.   *Tell why + what doing*

Sample Test Item(s):   Walter has been running for thirty minutes at seven miles per hour.
How much distance has he covered?   *word or two*

INSTRUCTIONAL ACTIVITY	CONTENT OF ACTIVITY	MEANS OF PRESENTING ACTIVITY
1. Motivation	Use highway travel and new speed limits.	Videotape & Teacher
2. Objective *Tell why + what*	Tell students they will solve word problems involving how far, fast, and long it takes to travel.	Teacher
3. Prerequisites *certain what need? skills?*	Assume math, travel. Remind that travel takes time, and how to use algebraic equation.	Teacher
4. Information and Examples *Our teaching (examples)*	Explain concepts of rate, time, and distance. Explain formula $D = R \times T$. Give examples involving each part of formula as the unknown.	Textbook & Teacher *How?*
5. Practice and Feedback *Limited Time*	Group students to work on variety of written problems. Review results with class, before individual practice.	Worksheet & Teacher
6. Testing *Brief*	Give a fifteen-item test, consisting of five problems solving for rate, time, and distance.	Worksheet
7. Enrichment and Remediation *→ meet + explain personally mention Books*	Pair students who mastered the objectives with those who did not. Students who mastered serve as tutors for those who did not.	Students

her students, the teacher has decided to show them a videotape of a public service announcement designed to inform people of the new state speed limits. Identify some of the questions the teacher should have asked herself before she decided to use this medium.

2.   Mrs. Brown usually has her students learn about the human circulatory system by having the students read a chapter in their textbook. However, this year she is teaching a group of below-average learners and she thinks they will not understand the textbook description. She decides that instead of having them read the textbook, she will give them a lecture in which she describes how the circulatory system works. She also decides that she will create some simple overhead transparencies. Was her selection of an alternative instructional medium a good one? Provide a rationale for your answer. Be sure that

your rationale deals with the issues of practicality, learner characteristics, and instructional activities.

3. Mr. Martinez is teaching the children in his kindergarten class to identify various shapes, and he feels they need more practice in this area. He decides that an appropriate solution to this problem will be to show the children an instructional film entitled *Ship-Shapes*. According to a promotional brochure he has read, the film focuses on the adventures of a famous cartoon character who "sails through the Land of Shapes and discovers the characteristics of the shapes he encounters there." Has Mr. Martinez chosen an instructional medium that is well suited for providing the practice he thinks his students need? Provide a rationale for your answer.

4. Mrs. Oliver usually has her students learn about parallel and series electrical circuits by having them read a chapter in their textbook. However, she has just read a review that says that "Circuit Maker" is an excellent computer game that focuses on this topic. She decides she will have her students play this game rather than read the description in the textbook. Do you think "Circuit Maker" is appropriate for the instructional purpose Mrs. Oliver has in mind? Provide a rationale for your answers.

5. Mr. Hinson has just read a brief review of a software program called "Compass Finder." According to the review, "'Compass Finder' is a computer simulation that gives students the opportunity to learn how to use a compass to help them find their way across unmarked terrain, and they never even have to leave the classroom!" Mr. Hinson would like his students to become proficient at using a compass, but he is skeptical about using computers for instructional purposes. Most of the instructional software he has seen could just as easily have been presented in print. Do you think that "Compass Finder" may be well suited for Mr. Hinson's instructional purposes? Provide a rationale for your answer.

FEEDBACK

1. Listed below are three general questions the teacher should have asked herself before she decided whether to use the videotape as part of her instructional plan. Listed beneath each general question are several more specific questions we think the teacher also should have asked. Don't be daunted by the number of questions we have listed; most of the questions related to choosing an instructional medium can be answered very quickly.

    A. Is the videotape practical to use in this situation?
        1. Is the videotape readily available?
        2. If the tape is not readily available, what will be the time and cost involved in obtaining it?
        3. Is a videotape player readily available?
        4. If a player is not readily available, what will be the time and cost involved in obtaining one?
        5. If there are expenses associated with showing the videotape, are there funds available to cover those expenses?
        6. Is there a convenient location in which the tape can be shown to my students?

    B. Is the videotape appropriate for my students?
        1. What attitudes are my students likely to have about being shown this videotape?

2. How will my students' attitudes affect their learning?
3. Does the videotape discuss the new speed limits in a manner that my students are likely to understand?

C. Is the videotape well suited to present the motivational activity for this lesson?
   1. Is the videotape likely to get my students thinking (gain their attention) about the new speed limits?
   2. Will the videotape, plus my comments, get the students interested in (arouse their curiosity about) figuring out how long it will now take to travel somewhere by car?

2. We agree with Mrs. Brown's decision to use overhead transparencies to help her describe how the human circulatory system operates. Let's discuss her decision in terms of the three factors we have focused upon in this chapter.

From a practical point of view, the time and cost involved in producing simple transparencies should be minimal. The necessary hardware (an overhead projector) is likely to be readily available and can easily be employed in the classroom.

The overhead transparencies Mrs. Brown intends to employ seem to be appropriate in light of the characteristics of her students. Using pictures to supplement an oral description of the human circulatory system seems like a good instructional decision regardless of the type of learner involved; however, such a decision seems to be particularly appropriate when dealing with below-average learners, who are less likely to grasp a concept that is only presented orally.

It also appears that the overhead transparencies, serving as supplements to Mrs. Brown's oral presentation, are appropriate for the instructional activity she has in mind. Obviously, Mrs. Brown's lecture is intended to provide her students with information and examples related to the human circulatory system. She can use her overhead transparencies to help her elaborate upon (present a visual model of) the information she presents during her lecture.

3. The instructional film Mr. Martinez has chosen to use does not seem to be well suited to provide his students with the practice he thinks they need. The film, as described in the quote from the promotional material, seems to present information about, and examples of, various shapes. However, there is no indication that the film will require the students to practice identifying shapes. Furthermore, when students are practicing an intellectual skill such as identifying shapes, it is important that they be given response-specific feedback. Even if practice opportunities were built into the film Mr. Martinez selected, the film would not be able to provide the students with such feedback.

4. Most instructional games are designed to simply provide students with practice in performing a particular skill; they are not usually intended to provide students with the information they will need in order to acquire that skill. Therefore, although the instructional game Mrs. Oliver has chosen may provide her students with excellent practice, it is unlikely that it will present them with the information they need to know about parallel and series circuits.

5. Simulations are programs designed to provide learners with a simplified model of some aspect of the real world and give the learners an opportunity to practice interacting with that model in a lifelike manner. Therefore, Mr. Hinson is likely to find that the simulation program he has read about will

present his learners with a chance to practice the skill he wants them to acquire without their having to leave the classroom. This practice opportunity cannot be provided by print materials. Mr. Hinson should seriously consider using the simulation as part of his instructional plan, which may, at a later point, also involve the students using a real compass.

APPLICATION

Choose the means you will use to present each of the instructional activities described in the two instructional plans you have been developing. List these "means of presentation" in the right-hand column of each plan. Be prepared to provide a rationale for each of instructional means you have chosen.

SUMMARY

In this chapter, we described how to decide whether to use a particular instructional medium as part of your instructional plan. Instructional media may be defined as the physical means (other than teacher, textbook, and supplementary print materials) by which instruction is delivered to students. The term "media hardware" refers to equipment, and the term "media software" refers to instructional materials presented via a piece of media hardware.

When you are choosing a means for presenting an instructional activity, in most cases you are likely to choose to present the activity yourself, via a textbook, or via supplementary print material such as a workbook. However, if you think you would like to use some other means to present the activity, you should ask yourself whether the medium you are considering will be (a) practical to use, (b) appropriate for your students, and (c) well suited to present a particular instructional activity.

In some cases, you will find that it is difficult to locate an instructional medium you consider suitable for delivering an instructional activity. In such cases, you will have to prepare your own materials. Methods of producing simple materials include writing, drawing, and creating. More complex mediated materials such as televised or computer-assisted instruction may also be produced.

One instructional medium that is becoming increasingly popular is the computer. Computer software can be grouped into four categories, each intended to serve a different purpose: drill-and-practice programs, tutorial programs, simulations, and instructional games. By being aware of the purposes different categories of software typically serve, you will be better able to decide whether a particular piece of software is an appropriate means of presenting a particular instructional activity.

CHAPTER NINE
IMPLEMENTING INSTRUCTION

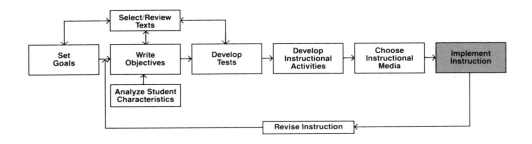

You developed an instructional plan for one or more objectives. This plan includes a brief description of each instructional activity you intend to present to your students. You analyzed these activities to determine which media would be used to support the instruction and, for those activities for which resources were not available, you described the types of materials that you might prepare. Now it's time to try your plan in the classroom.

PROBLEM SCENARIO

Mr. Vallano has just finished recording the grades for the posttest for a major unit in his college-prep math course. As he looks around the teachers' lounge, he wonders out loud why more students didn't do better on the exam. One of the teachers asks, "What's the problem?" Vallano indicates that the grades are more or less normally distributed. "That makes it a lot easier to assign grades," says his friend. Mr. Vallano thinks that this isn't a good enough answer. Somehow there has to be a better method to teach so that all of the students do well. How should he have implemented his instruction?

CHAPTER OBJECTIVE

The objective of this chapter is that you will be able to describe classroom practices that enhance student learning.

BACKGROUND INFORMATION

In this brief book, we can't teach you "how to teach" in the sense of how to interact with students. We cannot teach you the vast array of complex interpersonal skills that every teacher must develop in order to work effectively with students in the classroom. You will learn these skills in other courses and through your own classroom experiences. It is our view, however, that real teaching begins with the formulation of the instructional goals and objectives that serve as the basis for the development of an instructional plan. Without these elements, the teacher is at a loss in the classroom and becomes totally dependent upon the use of the textbook. In this chapter, we will describe systematic processes you can use in the classroom that will help every student learn as much as possible.

MAJOR CONCEPTS AND EXAMPLES

Much of the instruction that is presented in classrooms can be considered *group instruction*, that is, all the students participate in the same instructional activities at the same time. Since some students are able to learn more rapidly than others, the group-instruction approach usually results in a wide range of student performance. A few of the students do very well, a few do very poorly, and most of them end up somewhere in the middle.

In recent years, various attempts have been made to tailor instruction to the individual abilities of students. Most of these efforts have resulted in instruction that can be labeled *individualized instruction*. There are a number of ways to individualize instruction, such as allowing each student to proceed at his or her own pace, providing different instructional materials for different students, or allowing different students to work on different objectives. Almost all of these approaches result in serious classroom management problems. With so many students proceeding in so many different directions, it is almost impossible, even with the use of a computer, to keep track of individual students as they progress toward their individual instructional goals.

In addition to the management problems, many teachers who have taught in these situations note the strong desire of students to work together, whether it is in a small group or in a large group, under the direction of a teacher. Therefore, alternative approaches to total individualization have been proposed. One of the best known of these is the mastery learning approach proposed initially by Benjamin Bloom, an educator at the University of Chicago.

Mastery Learning Approach

Those who advocate the mastery learning approach make several basic assumptions about students who are engaged in the learning process. They assume that the reason some students do not achieve under the present system is that their aptitude limits the speed at which they can acquire new information. However, they indicate that nearly all students can master given instructional objectives if they are given enough time to do so, if the instruction they receive is of reasonable quality, and if they are tested frequently in order to determine if they are achieving mastery. Thus, mastery learning advocates propose that the basic distinction between the mastery learning approach and typical group instruction involves the amount of time students are given to acquire a set of objectives and the extent to which they acquire those objectives. Under the group-instruction approach, all students are given the same amount of time and, as a result, performances vary among students. Conversely, under the mastery learning approach, the time available to acquire a set of objectives varies among students and, consequently, most students eventually achieve about the same level of high performance.

Planning for Mastery Learning

Let's examine what must occur before a mastery learning approach can be implemented in the classroom. First of all, there usually is a set of learning objectives which all students are expected to achieve, and a set of test items which directly assess the behaviors described in the objectives.

Next comes a crucial step in planning for mastery learning—identifying the level of student performance that will constitute mastery. Those who have frequently used the mastery learning approach find that the best way to identify a mastery level of performance is to identify the level of performance of students who have received A's or B's in the past. Anything below that level is referred to as non-mastery. Therefore, a teacher might examine a twenty-item test, which has been designed to measure two objectives, and decide that a student must get at least eight out of ten items for each of the two objectives in order to achieve mastery. That decision might be based on the fact that previous students who had received an A or B in the course answered at least that many items correctly.

The next planning step is to combine sets of objectives so that teaching them requires as much as several weeks. After the objectives are clustered in this fashion, the teacher decides upon the instructional activities to employ when the instruction is initially presented to the students. This strategy usually includes some instruction that is presented to the entire class through group instruction. However, the teacher must also give considerable attention to the planning of individualized or small-group remedial and enrichment activities. The teacher must decide what kinds of materials and activities should be available for those students who do and do not reach mastery after the initial round of instruction. Given this level of preparation, the teacher is ready to implement a mastery learning approach to instruction.

Implementing a Mastery Learning Approach

Most students, at any grade level, are not accustomed to the mastery learning approach. Teachers who have used this method often find that it is necessary to conduct an orientation at the beginning of the course to stress that students will be graded only on the final exams at the end of major units and not on the more frequent intermediate tests. The students are also told that they will be graded on the basis of a fixed standard, and not in comparison with other students. They are told that they must reach certain standards to achieve mastery and that, in fact, all the students in the class can receive mastery grades if they all attain the specified level of performance for each portion of the course.

The students are also told that throughout the course they will receive intermediate formative examinations. The term *formative* refers to the fact that the information gained from the test will be used to diagnose the best remedial help for the student, if it is required. No decision is made or grades assigned based on the quality of the student's performance on these tests. Each student must also understand that he or she will receive all necessary help to meet the mastery criterion.

The teacher then begins to implement the instructional activities that have been prepared for the unit. After the group instruction for the unit has been presented, the teacher administers an objectives-based formative test. The students' scores on that test are used to determine who has mastered the unit and who has failed to do so. For those who have not mastered the instruction, various kinds of remedial activities are suggested. For those who have mastered the materials, alternative activities, including the tutoring of non-masters, are proposed.

When should the remedial instruction take place? During the first few weeks of a mastery learning course, it is almost always wise to provide the remedial activities during class time, immediately after the formative test results are known. This insures that students understand this is a regular and required part of the course. After the students have become accustomed to this practice, some, if not all, of the remedial activities can be assigned as homework, or a special period can be set aside each day for remediation.

You have just read about the basic approach to mastery learning. It is most interesting to note that in your instructional plan you have nearly all of the components required to implement such a strategy. You have the objectives, the assessment items, and the basic instructional approach. Perhaps the key element in the whole system is the remedial activities that follow the administration of a formative test. Research studies show that when mastery learning systems have failed, it has almost always been because of the failure of the teacher to follow up on the implementation of remedial strategies and on the reassessment of learners who initially failed to master a unit. Therefore, we can conclude that simply giving the formative examination and directing students to engage in remedial activities is not sufficient. We have to make sure that those remedial activities do, in fact, take place, that they are targeted on specific student deficiencies, and that we reexamine the students to certify that mastery has occurred. Without this step in the process, we will not be using the full capabilities of the mastery learning approach.

Sometimes it is difficult to determine what kinds of remedial activities will be effective for students who have not been able to master the objectives from the group instruction. Simply saying, "Go back and read the textbook again," has not proven very effective. What has proven effective is the use of peer tutors, older tutors, or small study group sessions in which each student has an opportunity to teach and be taught. Obviously, when remedial activities such as these are used, the teacher must have confidence in his or her ability to control students under such conditions because it can not be assumed that they will be highly motivated to participate in the remedial activities. To achieve this, it may be necessary to use various forms of rewards that are most appropriate for the students who are involved.

Results of Using the Mastery Learning Approach

Much research has been conducted in the last two decades on the use of the mastery learning strategy. In general, the results from that research indicate that typically two to three times as many students achieve mastery as previously achieved A's or B's in the course. That means that if in a traditionally taught course, 30 percent of the students are getting A's and B's, it would not be surprising to find that 60 percent to 90 percent of the students in a mastery learning course received A's and B's. It should be noted that these are perfectly legitimate, documented A's and B's that result from the alignment of objectives, tests, and instructional activities. The teacher is not giving out easy grades to students, but grades that students earn by their performance in relation to prespecified standards.

Those who use mastery learning in their classrooms have also found that students tend to have more positive attitudes toward the skills that are learned in this fashion. The one exception to this finding has been in those situations where the mastery learning standard has been set so high that students had to work beyond any reasonable level of expectation to achieve that level. When this occurred, attitudes toward the content have suffered accordingly.

Research results also suggest, but offer little firm evidence, that students may learn "how to learn" more effectively under mastery learning systems. When a mastery learning approach is used, students learn that there are ways of learning in school other than simply listening to the teacher and reading the textbook. They learn that they can learn from other students and that they, in turn, can help other students to learn. They also become more aware of the importance of objectives and how these relate to the assessment of their own learning. Some mastery learning advocates contend that with this new knowledge in hand, students are better able to direct their own study activities and thus they learn more, and do so in less time.

One of the other effects of using the mastery learning approach is the tendency for teachers to not only examine the performance of their students, but to also examine their own performance. In other words, by examining the extent to which students are successful or unsuccessful in achieving mastery, teachers become very aware of the quality of the instruction they are providing. Furthermore, by examining the performance and attitudes of their students, mastery learning teachers usually become quickly aware of the need to revise their instruction.

Alternative Teaching Approaches

While we have provided a detailed description of a mastery learning approach, it is certainly not the only one which is available to the teacher. The authors of this book, as well as many of the readers, were successfully educated using what would be considered a traditional teaching approach. Such an approach differs primarily in terms of less frequent objectives-based testing, and less concern for remediation of non-masters. Others have learned from less formal learning situations in which students are encouraged, especially at the primary level, to explore both physical stimuli and abstract symbols in order to discover new knowledge.

Critics of the traditional and discovery approaches argue that it is important to tell students what they are going to learn, and then to test them to see if they have. If they have not, then further help should be provided. We will not try to argue which approach is best; each has its merits. At different times with different objectives, different approaches may be required.

Of great importance in planning the implementation of instruction is to consider the feasibility of any given approach. Is there time and resources to use frequent testing and provide individualized feedback to students? If not, what compromises can be made? The answers to these questions will vary with each teaching situation. However, research has shown that the following activities seem to contribute the most to improving student learning:

- Indicating to students the expected standard of mastery (as opposed to having no pre-specified standards).
- Requiring students to take the time they need to master a skill.
- Giving frequent tests, with feedback.
- Assigning and grading homework.

These are major components of instructional practice that can be incorporated into a variety of approaches to classroom instruction. They will enhance the probability that students will learn, and that you, in turn, will be an effective teacher. If we reexamine the scenario in which Mr. Vallano was discouraged because of the fact that so few students did very well, we could suggest that he implement a mastery learning approach, or, at least incorporate standards, sufficient study time, and feedback to frequent tests and homework. These activities should enhance student performance.

PRACTICE

In this practice activity, we would like to have you consider the classroom setting in which you are likely to teach. Will it be possible to implement a mastery learning approach? We would not be surprised if your answer were no, because so many factors must be present for the entire approach to be used successfully. However, it may be possible to use some of the components of a mastery learning approach. The major components are listed here. Indicate if you would or would not use each component, and why.

1. Provide students with objectives that indicate what they must learn to do.
2. Present initial instruction to all students at one time.
3. Provide frequent tests on objectives.
4. Provide students with appropriate remedial activities.
5. Provide students with sufficient time to master instruction.
6. Provide students with frequent homework assignments that will be graded.

FEEDBACK

There is no specific feedback for this practice activity. However, we hope you find your analysis of classroom instructional practices to be helpful as you prepare the application activity described below.

APPLICATION

Select several of your instructional objectives and describe how a mastery learning strategy, or a modified strategy, could be used to implement your instructional plan for those objectives.

SUMMARY

In this chapter, we have described an instructional approach called the *mastery learning approach*. We have noted that such an approach usually begins with the identification of a set of specific objectives, the development of a set of test items designed to measure student attainment of the behaviors specified in those objectives, and the designation of the level of performance students must attain.

In mastery learning classes, each unit usually begins with some *group instruction*, including a formal presentation of information and ideas, as well as practice and feedback activities. Afterwards, students are given a formative test to determine if they have mastered the objectives for that unit. Those students who fail to master the objectives are given individualized or small group remedial instruction. Those students who have mastered the objectives are given enrichment activities that may include tutoring one or more of the students who had difficulty. After the students are given time for remediation, they are given another formative test to determine if they have now achieved mastery.

In this chapter we have also emphasized how you can use your instructional plan to implement mastery learning in your classroom. It was noted that the instructional plan, which includes objectives, sample test items, the instructional activities, media and textbook selection, as well as an indication of specific materials to be developed by the teacher, provides all the elements that are needed to implement a mastery learning strategy.

CHAPTER TEN
REVISING INSTRUCTION

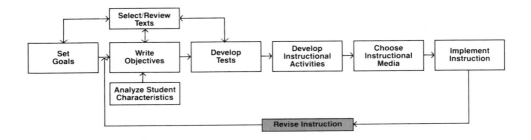

The systematic design of instruction does not end with the implementation of instruction. Useful information can be obtained from students that can be used to revise instruction so that it will be more effective the next time it is presented.

PROBLEM SCENARIO

Ms. Hatten has just about come to the conclusion that it is impossible to teach high school students about the involvement of the United States in the Middle East. She has taught this topic for the past three years, and each year has had increasing difficulty in getting students to understand the importance of U.S. participation in Middle Eastern affairs. The students seem to understand a few of the basic concepts, but then seem to get lost. Now Ms. Hatten is beginning to think that she should completely change her approach to this topic. How could she use data from the students to identify the problems they are having and how the instruction could be improved?

CHAPTER OBJECTIVES

The objectives for this chapter are that you will be able to

1. describe the types of information that should be collected from students during and after instruction which can be used to improve the instruction
2. interpret the data which have been collected from students and indicate how an instructional plan might be improved

BACKGROUND INFORMATION

Every teacher has had the experience of providing instruction that just did not work. Sometimes the problem with the instruction is obvious, but sometimes it is not. Our systematic view of instruction suggests that we must examine both the process of instruction, that is, what went on with the learners, as well as the results of the instruction, namely, the test performance and the attitudes of learners, in order to determine what went wrong and how it might be improved. It is important to note that this type of evaluation and revision is not focused on determining the value or worth of the instruction. It is a positive, constructive act that is considered a basic component of the teaching process, the purpose of which is to improve the instruction for future use.

When an instructional plan is prepared, many assumptions are made about such things as student skills, knowledge, and attitudes, and the appropriateness of the content and instructional activities to be employed. These are determined by our experience and knowledge of the students and the instructional setting. When instruction is implemented, it provides an opportunity to see just how well the lesson was designed and, of equal importance, how it can be improved for use the next time. If there is no intention of ever offering the instruction again, then there is no need to be involved in these systematic review and revision processes. However, since most instruction is given on a repeated basis, it is critically important to revise instructional plans so that they become more and more effective.

In Chapter Five we talked about developing test items that directly assess the objectives of your instruction, and in Chapter Nine we talked about implementing those tests in a mastery learning context in order to determine where students are having problems and how those problems might be remediated before they proceed. The same approach will be used in this chapter. Specifically, we will describe how information obtained from students can be used not only to improve their performance, but ultimately to improve the instruction for those who will receive it in the future.

MAJOR CONCEPTS AND EXAMPLES

In this section we will look at what data can be collected from students, when it can be collected, and how it should be interpreted and used to revise instruction. Data should be collected concerning student performance and student attitudes. There is an interesting relationship between these two sets of information. The basic outcomes of instruction are almost always stated in terms of the performance of learners, and without that performance, attitudes are of little consequence. However, in our attempts to get students to perform well, we must not forget about their attitudes. Often teachers are equally concerned with the attitudes of learners as they are with their performance. Having a learning situation in which students perform successfully, but do not have good feelings about the instruction, is certainly not satisfactory to many teachers because students are unlikely to want to study the topic in the future. Therefore we want to look at both performance and attitude.

What types of student performance are we referring to? Certainly we want to know what students know about a topic both before and after we teach them about it. However, if there is only one test, it should be based on the objectives for that lesson, and given at the end of the instruction.

Similar kinds of statements can be made about student attitudes. We would like to know what student attitudes are prior to instruction and afterwards. Student attitudes can be assessed with questionnaires, debriefing sessions after the instruction, or through observations of students during instruction.

How are performance data collected? As we have previously indicated, paper-and-pencil tests are usually employed to gather data concerning student performance on intellectual skills and knowledge objectives. Checklists or observation forms are often employed for motor skills and attitudinal outcomes.

When are the data collected? Ideally, data should be collected before, during, and after the instructional process. Information about students' attitudes and ability to perform one or more objectives should be collected prior to implementing a new instructional plan, if possible. It is also desirable to gather data during instruction. This can be done by looking at student performance on practice exercises. It can also be done by administering several brief quizzes designed to assess student progress toward acquisition of the objectives that are being taught. At the end of the instructional process, it is important to test the students to see if they have attained the objectives. In addition, some form of assessment of student attitudes should occur at this time. This assessment might be in the form of a questionnaire or a direct discussion with the students.

One other type of useful information is your own notes about what happened as you implemented the instructional plan. You will be working from your materials and will have a very good sense of what is and is not working at any given time. Be sure to document these kinds of reactions as they occur. They will become important to you later as you examine the test and attitude data and try to determine what went wrong and how instruction can be improved.

Listed below are the types of information you should consider collecting. They are listed as essential and additional information; the collection of the latter depending on the particular resources in the classroom.

Essential Information:

- Posttest on objectives
- Assessment of attitudes following instruction

Additional Information:

- Knowledge and attitudes prior to instruction
- Performance on exercises and tests during instruction
- Observation of students during instruction

Steps in Analyzing Information

After all the data have been collected, organize and review them systematically to identify what went right and what went wrong. Although this may seem like a major task, it really is not.

Begin your analysis by scoring the test you gave at the end of the instruction for the objectives covered by your instructional plan. As you are scoring the test, be sure that you examine the incorrect responses that the students are making, perhaps even noting them on a separate piece of paper. This information is helpful to you in two ways. First, it may help you identify misconceptions the students have as a result of your instruction. Once you identify such misconceptions, you can revise your instruction so that the next time you teach, the students will be unlikely to make the same mistakes. For example, young students might say that the sun is closer to the earth than the moon because it is brighter. This error could be dealt with directly the next time the lesson is taught.

Second, by noting the kinds of errors made by students, you should be able to detect defective test items—items that are not testing whether students have attained your objectives. How can you tell whether a test item is defective? For one, the nature of the incorrect responses often tell you whether students interpreted a question in the way in which you intended them to interpret it. Another indication is that a large number of the better students select the wrong answer. For the purposes of analyzing your instruction, student performance on defective items should be ignored, but the item should be revised if it is to be used again.

After you have scored the test and eliminated defective items, you should summarize the test data. This task can be made easier if you group

TABLE 9.1. Summary of Student Performance by Objective.

	1	2	3	4	Average
Art	100	100	100	100	100
Bob	100	75	100	25	75
Claire	100	100	100	75	94
Donna	75	75	75	75	75
Ernest	50	0	50	0	25
Frank	100	75	100	50	81
Gloria	100	100	100	100	100
Helen	75	100	50	25	63
Average	88	78	84	56	77

your test items by the objectives they measure. By doing so, you can easily determine how well your students performed on each objective. This information can then be put on a chart that lists each student's name down the left side and each objective across the top. By looking down the columns of the chart, you will be able to quickly tell how well your class was able to perform on each objective.

In the Table 9.1 you can see that eight students have taken a test which included items for four objectives. There were four items for each of the four objectives. You can use this table to identify those objectives students had difficulty with, and to review your instructional activities for those objectives. For example, of the objectives listed in Table 9.1, there certainly looks like there is a problem with objective four. For this objective it would be necessary to examine each component of the instructional plan to determine if it was appropriately planned and consistent with what we know about the type of desired learning outcome. Often in this retrospective phase, problems with instructional activities can be identified which were not apparent earlier. It is also necessary to examine the notes taken during the presentation of instruction. Do any of the problems seem to be related to the poor performance of students? For example, if it were noted that the students seemed to have problems with the practice exercises related to a particular objective, did they also have difficulty with the test items covering that objective?

After the test performance has been analyzed, it is important to take into consideration the attitudes students express toward the instruction. Did the students have a positive attitude about the instruction? If not, might poor performance on one or more objectives be related to the negative attitudes? How might the instructional plan be revised to improve student attitudes?

Revising the Instructional Plan

Let's examine the kinds of revisions that are often made at this point in the instructional process. First, as mentioned earlier, you may find that some of your test items must be revised because they do not measure the behaviors specified in your objectives. However, before you begin to revise your test items, it seems wise to review your objectives. Now that your instructional plan has been carried out and you have collected some data regarding its effectiveness, do you feel that your objectives can be achieved by your learners and that the objectives are appropriate for them? If the answer to both these questions is yes, then you should proceed with further refinement of your test items and other components of your instructional plan. If, however, you find the answer is no, then the first step is to reexamine each objective and either eliminate it or rewrite it at a higher or lower level, depending upon the capabilities of your learners.

The rewriting of the objectives subsequently results in revisions to your test items and your instructional activities, but this extra work is necessary if you are interested in having an instructional plan that is appropriate for future use. For example, did the motivational aspects of your instruction really work? Did they attract and maintain the learners' interest during the lesson? What about the information and examples you provided to the learners? In retrospect, does it appear that there was sufficient instruction here, and were the examples adequate for all learners? In other words, there may be several activities in the plan that could be revised.

Practice and feedback is often the instructional activity that can make or break a lesson. This instructional event may simply consist of students responding to worksheets or may involve student participation in a complex simulation. Regardless of the complexity of the activity, it is during this event that students practice performing the behavior that they are required to attain, and we hope, receive feedback regarding that performance. Without adequate practice and feedback, students typically have difficulty acquiring the behavior. Thus, if this portion of the lesson is inadequate, for whatever reason, it is quite likely to be reflected by poor performance on the posttest. Therefore, the analysis of student performance on the practice and feedback portion of your strategy is important because it shows if students mastered the objectives at that point.

The effectiveness of practice and feedback activities can also be assessed in terms of student performance on any quizzes that you administer as part of your instructional plan. Sometimes we find that students do quite well on these quizzes, but are unable to maintain that level of performance when they take a posttest. This seems to be particularly characteristic of below-average learners who can demonstrate immediate performance, but have a great deal of difficulty retaining information for a long period of time. The situation calls for a strategy of frequent review of existing knowledge and frequent testing of that knowledge.

The final area of concern is that of remedial activities. If you use the mastery learning strategy, undoubtedly some of your students will need remedial work. These are the students who are least likely, in the absence of remedial work, to be able to demonstrate mastery of the objectives that are part of your instructional plan. Therefore, the quality of your remedial activities has a major bearing on the performance of these students.

If you carefully examine your remedial activities, you may be able to identify ineffective approaches which, if changed, will enable most of your students to acquire your objectives. For example, in our problem scenario, Ms. Hatten required students who failed her short-answer tests in the unit on United States involvement in the Middle East to read a three-page summary she wrote and then respond to a series of true or false questions. After engaging in this remedial activity, the students were given another short-answer test on the subject. Only three of the seventeen students who received the remedial materials were able to pass the second test. Obviously, the remedial activity Ms. Hatten has developed was not successful. Considering the nature of the test she gave, perhaps Ms. Hatten should not only improve the instruction she provided, but also require her students to respond to short-answer questions, rather than true or false items, during the remedial activity. In addition, she might consider interspersing test items throughout her summary sheets, rather than putting all the items at the end.

Revising Instruction: An Example

Let's look at another fictitious scenario to see how an instructional unit might be revised. Jean Chen, a junior high school science teacher, has developed a unit that includes four objectives. The first three are knowledge objectives, one of which involves the recall of a formula; the fourth objective is an intellectual-skills objective that requires the students to use the formula to solve some problems.

Recently, Ms. Chen taught the unit for the first time. On Monday, she administered a pretest to the students and then gave them a lecture in which she presented the information related to the three knowledge objectives. On Tuesday, the class had a short discussion about the information that had been presented the previous day, and then were given a quiz over that information. On Wednesday, the students were shown a film, which demonstrated a procedure for conducting a laboratory activity, which involved the use of the formula the students had learned. After the film, the students who had passed the quiz were allowed to work on projects for the science fair while those students who failed were given a remedial information sheet to study and a worksheet to complete. On Thursday, Ms. Chen briefly reviewed the procedures that were to be used during the laboratory activity and then let the students conduct the exercise in the lab.

On Friday, the students finished the lab activity and were given a posttest covering all four objectives for the unit. Ms. Chen then held a "debriefing session" with the class, during which time she elicited their opinions about the new unit.

After the unit was over, Ms. Chen examined the data she had collected. The pretest scores revealed that the students knew virtually nothing about the topic beforehand. The quiz results indicated that 80 percent of the students were able to master the first three objectives by Tuesday. The other students were able to answer all of the questions on the remediation worksheet and were subsequently able to master the first three objectives on Friday's posttest. However, the posttest data revealed that only 50 percent of the students in the class were able to master the fourth objective.

Ms. Chen also reviewed the notes she had taken during the unit. Her perceptions were that Monday's lecture and Tuesday's class discussion had gone quite well. The film and the remedial activity that were presented on Wednesday also seemed to be effective. However, the laboratory activity that took place on Thursday and Friday seemed to have some problems. The lab apparatus broke down several times and the worksheets the students were supposed to use contained a number of misprints. These conditions seemed to frustrate a number of the students.

Ms. Chen's perceptions were confirmed by the opinions the students expressed during the debriefing session on Friday. For the most part, the students' opinions about the unit were quite positive. However, they indicated that they were frustrated about the laboratory activity, primarily because of the problems with the apparatus and worksheets, but also because they thought the activity seemed unrelated to the unit; using the formula they had been taught was only a very small part of the activity.

Given this information, Ms. Chen tried to decide how to revise her instructional plan for the unit. First of all, she examined the test items and found that they accurately reflected her objectives. Then she reexamined the objectives and decided they were appropriate for her students. Ms. Chen then looked at her instructional activities. The students seemed motivated throughout the unit, with the exception of their frustration with the laboratory activity. Apparently the information she had presented to the students was adequate—most of the students were able to master the knowledge objectives without any difficulty. Even those students who initially failed to master these objectives were able to do so after the remedial activity; thus, the remedial activity also seemed to be a good one. However, whereas all of the students were able to recall the formula she had taught them, only half of them were able to apply it to solve the problems that appeared on the posttest. Ms. Chen decided that during the unit she would have to provide more examples of how the formula could be used.

Most of the problems with the unit seemed to center around the laboratory exercise. Ms. Chen examined those portions of her unit related to the laboratory exercise. She decided that although the film seemed to clearly describe how to conduct the laboratory activity, the problems with the lab apparatus and worksheets obviously contributed to the students' sense of frustration. These problems would have to be resolved if the laboratory activity was conducted again. However, the students' comments about the lack of relevance of the laboratory activity led Ms. Chen to re-examine its appropriateness in relation to her objectives. In doing so, she decided that the next time she taught the unit she would change the labora-tory exercise to focus more directly on the formula she wanted her students to be able to use. As a result of this decision, she also had to find a replace-ment for the film she had used, as well as develop a different worksheet for the new laboratory activity. The lab apparatus her students would use for this activity would also be somewhat different from the apparatus that had been used the first time.

By examining the data she had collected, Ms. Chen decided to change her instructional plan for the unit in several fairly significant ways. Her objectives and tests would remain the same, as would her remedial activity and the first two days of her instructional activities. However, the film and laboratory exercises would be replaced. Furthermore, her revised plan would call for her to spend more time providing the students with exam-ples of how to use the formula they had memorized. Although these changes were rather substantial, Ms. Chen was eager to make them, feeling that they would result in making her instruction more effective.

Other Considerations

Before concluding our discussion of revising instruction, two points will be considered related to grading students and using mastery learning data. First, with regard to grading students, there are a variety of approaches that can be used, all of which have their strengths and weak-nesses. The most important point is that by using objectives-referenced tests, you have a good indication of exactly what each student can and can not do. This information can be used to determine an equitable and fair assessment of each student.

Lastly, you have probably noticed the relationship between the use of a mastery learning strategy or some variation of that strategy, and the collection of data and information that is useful for revising instruction. The frequent testing of students on the objectives provides the data required to identify instructional problems. This data, along with posttests, and observations and discussions with the students can be invaluable in identifying what should be revised, and how it should be revised.

PRACTICE

1. Assume that you are responsible for teaching a high school career education class. There are twenty-two students in the class. One of the major objectives of the class is that the students will be able to successfully complete an application form for a job. You prepare and implement an instructional plan for the objective. Describe the various types of data and information you would collect in order to evaluate and revise the instructional plan.

2. Mr. Lyons, a physical education major, has been hired as a new teacher at a local elementary school. His first assignment is to teach a unit of physical fitness. It seems that the unit was taught last year to some fourth graders and data have been collected. Mr. Lyons' responsibility is to understand how the unit was taught and revise the methodology before teaching it next week.

   Mr. Lyons finds that there are three major objectives related to the physical fitness goal: (a) students will be able to do five consecutive push-ups, (b) students will be able to do two consecutive chin-ups, and (c) students will be able to run a quarter mile in four minutes.

   The plan used by the instructor who previously taught the unit indicated that he motivated the students by telling them how important it is to be physically fit. Subsequently, he showed the students how to do push-ups and chin-ups, and simply told them they would have to be able to run around the track in four minutes or less. After this instruction, the students were organized into groups and spent the next several days practicing each of the three objectives. At the end of the week, each student was individually tested on the three objectives. The results were as follows:

   A. five push-ups: 80 percent of the students were successful
   B. two chin-ups: 30 percent of the students were successful
   C. run a quarter mile in four minutes: 50 percent of the students were successful.

   When the teacher talked with the students about the instruction, there were a great variety of reactions, ranging from those who were very enthusiastic to those who thought it was extremely poor. Mr. Lyons now must decide what to do with all of this information.

   Based on the scenario, answer the following questions:

   A. How would you examine the data and information the previous teacher provided for Mr. Lyons?
   B. What do the data tell you about the effectiveness of the previous teacher's instructional plan?
   C. If you were Mr. Lyons, how would you change the instructional plan before you taught the unit?

FEEDBACK

For the two practice activities in this chapter, your answers may be somewhat different from ours, but should cover many of the same points.

1. Below is a description of the types of data and information we would collect if we were evaluating an instructional plan designed to teach students how to successfully complete a job application.

    First, on the day we began teaching this topic, we would try to ascertain the basic reading and writing competencies of the students and the extent to which they were already able to fill out a job application form from a local company.

    Second, during the instruction we would have a practice activity which would involve having the students fill out a job application form. When we evaluated our instructional plan, we would want to know how well the students were able to fill out this form. The information we gather should give us a good indication of the effectiveness of the instruction delivered prior to practice exercises.

    Third, we would administer a posttest that was similar to the pretest. In other words, on the posttest, the students would again be required to fill out a job application form. This form would not be the same one that was used on the pretest, nor would it be the same as the form used during the practice exercise. Student performance on this test would give us a good indication of the success of our instructional strategy, including the practice, feedback, and remedial activities.

    Fourth, at the end of the unit, we would ask the students to respond to a very brief questionnaire in which we would ask them about any problems they had with the instruction and the posttest. We would also ask them about their attitudes toward the instruction.

    Fifth, we would take notes concerning our delivery of the instruction, as well as our perceptions regarding student responses to the instruction.

    By collecting all of these types of data, we should be able to evaluate the effectiveness of our instruction, as well as identify those sections of the instructional plan that should be revised.

2. Listed below is a description of how Mr. Lyons went about examining and interpreting the data the previous teacher provided for him, and how he went about changing the instructional plan for the unit. It just so happens that Mr. Lyons, having recently read this book, performed each of these tasks in an exemplary manner! Therefore, we hope that your response is similar to what is described below.

    The first thing Mr. Lyons did was examine whether the assessment activities the previous teacher employed measured the behaviors described in the objectives for the unit. Having found that they did, he checked the literature from the President's Council on Physical Fitness to make sure that the objectives were appropriate for the students, and he determined that they were.

    Next, Mr. Lyons reviewed the data that were collected when the previous teacher assessed the students at the end of the unit. Since at the end of the unit, only 30 percent of the students were able to do two chin-ups and only 50 percent of the students were able to run a quarter mile in four minutes, the unit was judged not to be very effective. Furthermore, Mr. Lyons was not particularly impressed by the fact that by the end of the lesson, 80 percent of the students were able to do five push-ups. He reasoned that since the students were not pretested, it was impossible to tell whether the students might have been able to perform this feat before instruction. If they already were, then the unit was quite unsuccessful.

    When Mr. Lyons reviewed the comments the students made regarding their reactions to the unit, he concluded that perhaps the wide range of opinions expressed by the students reflected their general attitudes toward physical fitness and that the instructional unit had little, if any, effect on those attitudes.

Having analyzed the data the previous teacher provided for him, and having decided that the unit had very little effect on student performance and attitudes, Mr. Lyons decided that he would make some extensive revisions in the instructional plan before he taught the unit. Since the objectives and assessment activities for the unit seemed appropriate, Mr. Lyons decided that other than adding a pretest, he would not change these. However, when he reviewed the various activities that comprised the instructional plan for the unit, he decided that a number of major changes were in order.

First, he concluded that although the three objectives for the unit involved motor skills, the chances that the children would acquire those skills would be greatly increased if they had positive attitudes about being physically fit. He felt the children were unlikely to acquire a positive attitude simply by having their instructor tell them how important it was to be fit. Therefore, he decided to begin the unit with a film in which a role model for the children demonstrated the motor skills and briefly discussed the benefits of being physically fit. In addition, Mr. Lyons decided that when he taught the children how to perform these skills, he would have them demonstrated by children who passed the pretest or by respected children from the next higher grade. He decided to do this because he felt that the students would be encouraged to perform the skills if they saw them performed by other children they admired.

Mr. Lyons also decided that during the days that the students would be practicing the skills, he would set up three "check-out stations" to assess individual student progress toward attainment of the three objectives. At first, he and the students who passed the pretest would be the evaluators at the three stations. As more students demonstrated mastery of the objectives, they would be asked to help at the stations and assist some of the other students. Thus, Mr. Lyons would have more time to work with those students who were having the most difficulty. He felt that by using these procedures while the students were practicing the skills, he would greatly increase the chances that a much larger percentage of the students would acquire the skills by the end of the unit and, hopefully, would have better attitudes toward physical fitness.

APPLICATION

Describe the plan you will use for collecting data and information to revise the instructional plan you developed in the previous chapter. Indicate what data and information you will collect, when you will collect it, and how you will collect it. Also indicate how that information will be used to identify problems and subsequently to revise your instructional plan.

SUMMARY

In this chapter, we have encouraged you to prepare for the possibility that your instructional plan will not work perfectly the first time. In order to revise it, we suggested that basic information on student performance and attitudes should be collected prior to, during, and after the implementation of instruction. Likewise, your own observations of the effectiveness of various components of your instructional plan will be of great value.

After the instruction, the data for each of your objectives should be summarized. In doing so, you verify that your test items accurately assessed the behaviors specified in your objectives and that your objectives were appropriate ones. In those cases where many students failed to attain an objective, a review of the various components of your instructional plan for that objective is necessary. You must determine what revisions are needed before the next implementation of your instructional plan.

CHAPTER ELEVEN
PLANNING EFFECTIVE INSTRUCTION: A SUMMARY

In his book, *Teachers and Machines,* Larry Cuban has described today's public school classroom. Cuban is a former teacher and administrator who has attempted to analyze why teachers have not chosen to use technology in the classroom to a greater extent than they have. Read this excerpt from Cuban's book, part of which you may remember from Chapter One, and see if you agree with his description of the classroom.

The classroom, located within the larger school organization, is a crowded setting in which the teacher has to manage twenty-five or more students of approximately the same age who involuntarily spend—depending upon their grade level—anywhere from one to five hours daily in a room. Amidst continual communication with individual students and groups (up to 1,000 interactions a day in an elementary classroom), the teacher is expected to maintain control, teach a prescribed content, capture student interest in that content, match levels of instruction to differences among students, and show tangible evidence that students have performed satisfactorily.

Within these overlapping school and classroom settings, the argument runs, teachers have rationed their time and energy to cope with conflicting and multiple demands and have constructed certain teaching practices that have emerged as resilient, simple, and efficient solutions in dealing with a large number of students in a small space for extended periods of time.

So, for example, rows of movable desks and seating charts permit the teacher easy surveillance of the room. The teacher's desk, usually located in a visually prominent part of the room near a chalkboard, underscores quietly who determines the direction for what the class will do each day. Class routines for students, such as raising their hands to answer questions, speaking only when recognized by the teacher, and speaking when no one else is talking, establish an orderly framework for group instruction. Teaching the entire class at one time is simply an efficient and convenient use of the teacher's time—a valuable and scarce resource—in covering required content and maintaining control. Lecturing, recitation, seatwork, and homework drawn from texts are direct, uncomplicated ways of transmitting knowledge and directions to groups. Given the constraints placed upon the teacher by the daily schedule and the requirements that a course of study be completed by June, these instructional practices permit the teacher to determine, in a timely and efficient manner, whether or not students have learned the material.*

We believe that Cuban has accurately described the classrooms of America today. And, although we hope that the future will result in some changes in the portrait, the picture Cuban has painted may serve as an accurate portrayal of the typical American classroom for many years to come.

Regardless of whether the typical classroom scenario changes or remains the same, teachers will find it easy to use the approach to teaching that we have described in this book because the approach recognizes the realities of the environment in which teaching takes place. And, perhaps even more importantly, the approach encourages the use of instructional practices which, according to research, are most likely to be effective. In short, we believe that the approach we have described in this book is both practical and effective.

We would like to review what we believe are the three major themes that run throughout this book. The first is that effective instruction is a result of systematic planning. The chapters in this book have focused on the steps in that planning process. The second theme is that rather than viewing student learning as a single entity, teachers should recognize that there are a variety of different types of learning outcomes and that effective instructional plans will differ depending upon the type of outcome they want their students to attain. The third theme is that the instructional approach we employ may have to be modified based upon the characteristics of our learners. Let's review these three themes in a summary fashion.

*Larry Cuban. *Teachers and Machines*. New York: Teachers College Press, 1986, pp. 57–58.

SYSTEMATIC STEPS FOR PLANNING EFFECTIVE INSTRUCTION

Effective instruction must be derived from goals. Although the goals will be established in a variety of ways, each goal must be translated into something meaningful to the classroom teacher. Specifically, goals should be translated into objectives which express what it is that students will be able to do and how well they will be able to do it. It may be necessary to modify, add, or delete some of our objectives based upon knowledge of the general ability, attitudes, and specific skills which our learners possess. The objectives provide the stimulus for the development of test items and other assessments that measure the extent to which the behaviors described in the objectives have been achieved by our students.

Based on our knowledge of our objectives and of our students, we can develop an instructional plan to take into the classroom. The instructional plan must take into consideration ways of motivating learners, informing them of the objectives they will have to achieve, and reminding them of the prerequisite skills and knowledge they should possess. In addition, the plan should indicate the information and examples that will be presented to students and the various types of practice and feedback activities available to them. Finally, the type of testing that will take place, as well as any types of remediation and enrichment activities that will be available for students, should be described.

Based on the objectives and the instructional activities described in the plan, we can select the appropriate media and text materials to support those activities. At times, it will be necessary to develop materials for certain activities for which resources can not be located.

After our plan has been developed and our resources have been selected, it is time to implement the activities with students. We have proposed that a successful strategy for working with students in the classroom is that of mastery learning. Inasmuch as a great deal of the instructional activities in a mastery learning classroom can be group-based, this strategy does not deviate in a significant fashion from many of the techniques already used by teachers. However, it does involve frequent testing of students and the provision of feedback and remedial instruction related to the objectives with which students are having difficulty.

The instructional plan you develop can be implemented in a variety of ways. However, we believe that the mastery approach is a valuable instructional method. Research indicates that when this approach is effectively implemented in the classroom, overall student performance is greatly enhanced and students may gain the additional benefit of developing new learning-how-to-learn skills.

The tests that students take to demonstrate their ability to perform the behaviors described in our objectives also produce information that can be used to improve our instruction. The test data and attitudinal information we collect help pinpoint defective areas in the instructional plan and serve as the basis for deciding upon ways in which the plan may be improved prior to implementing it in the future.

IMPORTANCE OF THE DOMAINS OF LEARNING OUTCOMES

Throughout this book, we have focused on instructional goals and objectives that describe things learners should know or should be able to do. Furthermore, we have indicated that goals and objectives should not be viewed as a single entity. Instead, it is important to identify the type of learning outcome each goal or objective represents. We have indicated that goals and objectives can be classified into four categories, or domains: knowledge, intellectual skills, motor skills, and attitudes. The importance of identifying the learning domain of a goal or objective lies in the fact that certain instructional activities vary in their importance depending upon the domain of the objective.

IMPORTANCE OF STUDENT CHARACTERISTICS

We have emphasized that all the students in our classrooms are not the same. Students are often identified as being below average, average, or above average. Teachers who work with these categories of students know that they can be quite different in terms of their attitudes toward learning and their ability to perform a given learning task. Therefore, our content and our instructional approach may need modification based on our learners' abilities and attitudes.

CONCLUSION

The approach to teaching described in this book is based on both theory and research. However, much remains to be learned about how to facilitate the learning process, and that knowledge is likely to be discovered both in the research laboratory and in the classroom. Because we are still in the process of learning about learning, we urge you not to view any of the ideas we have expressed in this book as being cast in concrete. Instead, we hope that you will consider our ideas and adapt them for use in your own instructional setting.

What we do hope you will maintain is the perception of the critical interrelationship of all the things we do in the classroom. That, in fact, our objectives should be derived from goals, our tests should be based on the behaviors described in our objectives, and our instructional activities should be targeted on the behaviors described in our objectives and assessed on our tests. We also hope that you will recognize the value of gathering data and information about the effectiveness of your instruction, and that throughout your teaching career you will gather and use such data to revise and improve your instruction.

Teachers must make many, many decisions during their professional careers. A number of those decisions involve the planning and implementation of instruction. We have provided you with various tools to help you make good decisions about these matters. We hope that effective instruction will be the result.

Carefully consider the ideas presented in this book and use them in a manner which will meet your needs. Regardless of the choices you make, we hope that you will be successful as a teacher. May all of your students be masters!

GLOSSARY

Note: We have attempted to define the terms listed in this glossary in accordance with the way the terms were used in this book. Many of the terms have other meanings in other contexts.

ATTITUDE. A type (or domain) of learning outcome that focuses upon the personal choices of students. These choices are based upon students' feelings and beliefs.

BEHAVIOR. That component of an objective which describes what the students will be expected to do, that is, the observable action they will be expected to take, as a result of instruction.

CHECKLIST. A set of criteria used for judging the adequacy of a students' performance. The criteria often consist of descriptions of the characteristics of a successful performance. Checklists are usually used to assess students' attainment of motor skills.

CONCEPT. A label used to describe a group of related things or ideas. Examples of concepts include "chair," "dictatorship," "planet," "red," and so on.

CONCEPT LEARNING. A type of learning outcome (within the intellectual skills domain) that focuses on the ability to identify whether specific things or ideas can be classified as examples of a particular concept.

CONDITIONS. That component of an objective which describes the circumstances under which a student will be expected to perform a desired behavior.

CRITERION. That component of an objective which describes how well (and perhaps, how quickly) a student will be expected to perform a desired behavior.

CRITERION-REFERENCED TEST. *See* **OBJECTIVE-REFERENCED TEST.**

DRILL-AND-PRACTICE PROGRAM.   An instructional program, presented by a computer, designed to provide students with the opportunity to practice skills or to rehearse knowledge previously presented to them.

EFFECTIVE INSTRUCTION.   Instruction that enables students to acquire specified skills, knowledge, and attitudes, and which students enjoy.

ENRICHMENT.   Instructional activities intended to extend student knowledge or skills beyond that which is required.

EXAMPLES.   Instances depicting the proper performance of a given behavior.

EXECUTIVE ROUTINE.   The series of steps that must be followed in the process of performing a motor skill.

FEEDBACK.   The information a student receives regarding the answer or answers he or she provided. At a minimum, feedback lets the student know whether the answer was correct. In addition, feedback may indicate what the correct answer was, why it was correct, and, perhaps, what was wrong with the student's incorrect answer.

FORMATIVE EXAMINATION.   A type of test, used as a component of the mastery learning approach, designed to assess student progress toward attainment of a given set of objectives. Students' grades are not affected by their performance on this type of test.

GOALS.   Statements of desired outcomes of instruction, usually described in general terms. Goals may focus on outcomes related to schools, teachers, or students.

GROUP INSTRUCTION.   The process by which all the students in a class participate in the same instructional activities at the same time.

INDIVIDUALIZED INSTRUCTION.   Instruction tailored to the individual abilities of students. Means of individualizing instruction include allowing each student to proceed through instruction at his or her own pace, providing different instructional materials for different students, and allowing different students to work on different objectives.

INFORMATION.   The content (substance) a student needs to know in order to be able to attain a given objective.

INSTRUCTIONAL ACTIVITIES.   The steps (events) that take place when instruction is presented to students.

INSTRUCTIONAL DESIGN.   A systematic process for designing, developing, implementing, and evaluating instruction.

INSTRUCTIONAL GAME.   An instructional program, presented by the computer, designed to have students practice performing a particular skill in the context of a game.

INSTRUCTIONAL PLAN.   A brief description of the goals, objectives, test items, and instructional activities for a given segment of instruction.

INTELLECTUAL SKILL.   A type (or domain) of learning outcome that focuses on the ability to use, rather than simply state, information. Types of intellectual skills include concept learning, rule using, and problem solving.

KNOWLEDGE.   A type (or domain) of learning outcome that focuses on the ability to recall and state specific information.

LEARNING OUTCOMES.   Descriptions of what students should be able to do as a result of instruction. This term may either refer to objectives or to goals that focus upon student behaviors.

MASTERY.   A level of performance (with respect to a particular objective or set of objectives) considered to be satisfactory or better.

MASTERY LEARNING APPROACH.   An instructional approach under which the instructional time spent on a set of objectives varies among students so that most students eventually attain all of the objectives. Underlying the mastery learning approach is the theory that nearly all students can master a given set of instructional objectives if they are allowed enough time to do so, if the instruction they receive is of a reasonable quality, and if they are tested frequently in order to determine whether they are achieving mastery.

MEDIA.   The physical means (other than the teacher, textbook, and supplementary print materials) by which instruction is delivered to students.

MEDIA HARDWARE.   The equipment, such as computers, televisions, and tape players, that is used to present mediated materials (media software).

MEDIA SOFTWARE.   The instructional materials that are presented using a piece of media hardware.

MEDIATED MATERIALS.   *See* **MEDIA SOFTWARE.**

MOTOR SKILL.   A type (or domain) of learning outcome that focuses upon the ability to perform a physical activity.

OBJECTIVE-REFERENCED TEST.   A test designed to measure student ability to perform the behaviors specified in a given set of objectives. This type of test is also known as a criterion-referenced test.

OBJECTIVES.   Explicit statements of what students will be able to do at the end of a segment of instruction.

PRACTICE.   The opportunity students are given to perform a particular behavior prior to the time when they are tested.

PREREQUISITE SKILLS.   The skills, knowledge, and attitudes students must possess in order to be ready for (capable of understanding) instruction on related skills, knowledge, or attitudes.

PROBLEM SOLVING.   A type of learning outcome (within the intellectual skills domain) that focuses upon the ability to choose, as well as use, the rules needed to solve a particular problem. For example, a student who solves a word problem in mathematics without being told what rules to use in order to solve the problem is said to have engaged in problem solving.

REMEDIATION.   Instructional activities designed to enable students to attain an objective that they were unable to attain previously.

RULE.   A description of a means of arriving at a solution to a particular type of problem. Rules usually are composed of a combination of concepts. An example of a rule would be "when adding two fractions with the same denominator, add the two numerators and place them over the common denominator."

RULE USING.   A type of learning outcome (within the intellectual skills domain) that focuses upon the ability to use a given rule to solve a particular type of problem.

SIMULATION.   An instructional program, presented by the computer, designed to provide students with a simplified model of some aspect of the real world and give the student the opportunity to interact with that model in a real-life manner.

SOCIAL FAIRNESS.   The belief that textbooks and other instructional materials should represent individuals in various age, ethnic, and racial groups, as well as members of the two sexes, as being equal in society, without preenting any stereotypes in terms of interests, abilities, occupations, physical appearances, or languages.

SKILL-ALIGNMENT CHECK.   The process of determining whether there is congruence between instructional objectives, instructional content, and tests. In other words, the process of determining whether the skills specified in a given set of objectives are the same skills as those being taught and those being tested.

SKILLS TRACE.   *See* **SKILL-ALIGNMENT CHECK.**

STANDARD. *See* **CRITERION.**

TUTORIAL PROGRAM. An instructional program, presented by a computer, designed to provide students with instructional information and examples related to a given objective. The program may also provide students with the opportunity to practice the behavior specified in the objective.

VALIDITY. A test item or test is considered to be valid (to possess validity) if it measures the behavior (that is, knowledge, skill, or attitude) it was intended to measure.

BIBLIOGRAPHY

GENERAL REFERENCES

DICK, W., and L. M. CAREY, 1985. *The Systematic Design of Instruction.* 2d ed. (Glenview, Ill.: Scott Foresman).

GAGNE, R. M., 1985. *The Conditions of Learning.* 4th ed. (New York: Holt, Rinehart and Winston).

————. ed., 1987. *Instructional Technology: Foundations.* (Hillsdale, N.J.: Lawrence Erlbaum Associates).

GAGNE, R. M., L. J. BRIGGS, and W. WAGER, 1988. *Principles of Instructional Design.* 3d ed. (New York: Holt, Rinehart and Winston).

GAGNE, R. M., and M. P. DRISCOLL, 1988. *Essentials of Learning for Instruction.* 2d ed. (Englewood Cliffs, N.J.: Prentice-Hall).

KNIRK, F. G., and K. L. GUSTAFSON, 1986. *Instructional Technology: A Systematic Approach to Education.* (New York: Holt, Rinehart and Winston).

SULLIVAN, H., and N. HIGGINS, 1983. *Teaching for Competence.* (New York: Teachers College Press).

TILLMAN, M., D. BERSOFF, and J. DOLLY, 1976. *Learning to Teach: A Decision-Making System.* (Lexington, Mass.: D.C. Heath).

SPECIAL TOPICS

ALESSI, S. M., and S. R. TROLLIP, 1985. *Computer-Based Instruction: Methods and Development.* (Englewood Cliffs, N.J.: Prentice-Hall).

BLOCK, J. H., H. E. EFTHIM, and R. B. BURNS, 1989. *Building Effective Mastery Learning Schools.* (New York: Longman).

BLOOM, B. S., 1956. *Taxonomy of Educational Objectives: Cognitive Domain.* (New York: David McKay).

————. 1976. *Human Characteristics and School Learning.* (New York: McGraw-Hill).

————. 1981. *All Our Children Learning.* (New York: McGraw-Hill).

CAREY, L. M., 1988. *Measurement and Evaluation of School Learning.* (Boston: Allyn and Bacon).

CUBAN, L., 1986. *Teachers and Machines: The Classroom Use of Technology Since 1920.* (New York: Teachers College Press).

HANNAFIN, M. J., and K. C. PECK, 1988. *The Design, Development and Evaluation of Instructional Software.* (New York: Macmillan).

KAUFMAN, R., 1979. *Needs Assessment: Concept and Application.* (Englewood Cliffs, N.J.: Educational Technology Publications).

MAGER, R. F., 1984. *Preparing Instructional Objectives.* Rev. 2d ed. (Belmont, Calif.: Pitman Learning).

MARTIN, B. L., and L. J. BRIGGS, 1986. *The Affective and Cognitive Domains: Integration for Instruction and Research.* (Englewood Cliffs, N.J.: Educational Technology Publications).

REIGELUTH, C. M., 1983. *Instructional Design Theories and Models: An Overview of Their Current Status.* (Hillsdale, N.J.: Lawrence Erlbaum Associates).

REISER, R. A. and R. M. GAGNE, 1983. *Selecting Media for Instruction.* (Englewood Cliffs, N.J.: Educational Technology Publications).

TILLMAN, M., 1982. *Troubleshooting Classroom Problems.* (Glenview, Ill.: Scott Foresman).